MEDIEVAL LAW TEACHERS AND WRITERS

COLLECTION DES TRAVAUX DE LA FACULTÉ DE DROIT
DE L'UNIVERSITÉ D'OTTAWA

Monographies juridiques n° 9

ISBN-0-7766-2014-2

MEDIEVAL LAW TEACHERS AND WRITERS

Civilian and Canonist

by

J.A. CLARENCE SMITH
M.A. (Cantab.), Barrister-at-Law (Middle Temple)
Professor of Law at the University of Ottawa

University of Ottawa Press
Ottawa, Canada
1975

Preface

THE GENESIS of this guide-book lies in the exasperation which I experienced when collecting and translating medieval texts on the Conflict of Laws — still in progress — at the difficulty of identifying the predecessors whom every writer diligently cites. A stimulus was added by a suggestion from Erwin Surrency when he published my translation of Bartolo on the Conflict of Laws,[1] to the effect that a "series of vignettes" might be of more general interest.

For the medieval resuscitation, development and adaptation of Roman law was the work of a succession of individual writers, mostly university professors. Who they were and how they worked is the framework of the development itself; but serious attention has not often been paid to this question,[2] least of all in English. The labour of many men's love, mainly in this century, has replaced bit by bit with sober documented truth the mass of fable snowballing down from writer to uncritical writer; but there are still gaps, and the greater part of what has been achieved lies locked in publications difficult to find. Even when found their understanding requires, if not a polyglot, at least one at home in the tower of Babel in which the loss of Latin has imprisoned modern scholarship. It is however a story to which allusion is not infrequently made, and not always very accurately.[3] The object of this overall view is to reduce the mystification which the non-specialist feels when confronted with such references: there is little

---

1. (1970) 14 American Journal of Legal History 157 to 183 and 247 to 275.
2. The earliest surviving collection of notices was made by Giambattista CACCIALUPI in 1467 (paragraph 153 below). Much more voluminous was the work of an industrious Greek, Thomas DIPLOVATATIUS in 1511; and in 1769-72 Dom Mauro SARTI examined critically the lives of Bolognese teachers. There were other works dealing with other law-schools, all in Latin, and relying almost entirely on the teachers' own writings. In the middle of the nineteenth century Friedrich Carl von SAVIGNY added (in German) to all these a fair amount of evidence from contemporary records. His second edition (1850 for the volumes that interest us) was considerably more informative than the first, and this second edition was quickly translated into Italian. The only French translation of the volumes relevant to this study is of the first edition; and the only English translation is of the first edition and of the first volume which does not interest us here.
3. The present writer pleads guilty to having himself repeated a few of the current inaccuracies in the introduction (pages 157 to 159) to his translation of Bartolo on the Conflict of Laws (note 1 above). He has at least erred in good company: Dean Gabriel LE BRAS on the civilian glossators, at pages 30 to 37 of *l'Age Classique* (1965) and elsewhere, is little better than slapdash.

original in it, except the arrangement, but on the occasions when I have consulted a manuscript myself the reference is accompanied by the conventional asterisk.

A word is necessary on the form in which the writers' names appear. It would have been easy — and would avoid shocking the specialist — simply to keep them in the Latin dress which they wear in their Latin writings. But this would go towards perpetuating the mystification which this book sets out to remove: the professors in question were ordinary human beings with (for the most part) ordinary names, and their names do not look ordinary unless translated into English. French and Italian legal historians do not scruple to translate names into their respective languages; nor do English historians other than legal, whether their sources are in Latin or in any other tongue, and whether their characters are exalted or humble. The few names which are not ordinary have been left in Latin, and in every other case the latinised form is added in brackets unless it is simply the addition of *-us*. Inevitably some of the equivalents are less happy than others, particularly in the field of surnames: it is in fact deceptive to show as surnames what were (at the beginning of this period) patronymics or nicknames. A third kind of addition to the personal name is "of" and a place: this nearly always indicates the place of birth, but with a churchman might be the place of his benefice. Noble surnames have been left in Italian; and when, after 1250, surnames appear in the form typified (for English readers) by *dei* or *de' Medici* (in Latin *de Medicis* or *Medicus*, the latter sometimes italianised to *Medico*), they have been modernised by the omission of *dei*, *de'* or *degli*.

In my spelling of Latin words I have oscillated between the classical "ae" and the medieval "e:" the benevolent reader will perhaps detect a system.

It would not have been possible to write this book without the aid of the Inter-Library Loan Service of the Ottawa University Library: my particular thanks are due to Madame Daoust who has been in charge of this service. And it would not have been possible to print it without a grant from the Canadian and Foreign Law Research Centre of the Faculty of Law, Ottawa University.

J.A. Clarence Smith

Ottawa,

Table of contents

Analytical Table of Paragraphs

Chapter I. — **Prologue: the Setting of the Scene**

Chapter II. — **First Steps: Text, Gloss, Treatise**

Chapter III. — **Overall Views: the Summa**

Chapter IV. — **The Zenith: Definitive Summa, Standard Gloss**

Chapter V. — **Italian Pause: "Additio", "Questio", "Disputatio"**

Chapter VI. — **French Interlude: "Repetitio", "Lectura Reportata"**

Chapter VII. — **Maturity: the Commentary**

Chapter VIII. — **Decline: "Consilia"**

Chapter IX. — **Mediocrity: More "Consilia", French Customs**

Chapter X. — **Epilogue: New Learning**

Abbreviations

[Contributions to Dictionaries and Encyclopedias are cited in the same way as articles, by contributor's name, title, year and number of volume, and page.]

ALIDOSI — Giovanne Nicolò Pasquale ALIDOSI, *Li Dottori Bolognesi di Legge Canonica e Civile* (1620).

BELLOMO — Manlio BELLOMO

Due Libri Magni — *Due Libri Magni Quæstionum Disputatarum,* (1969) 81 Studi Senesi 256.

Una famiglia — *Una famiglia di giuristi: i Saliceti di Bologna,* (1969) 81 Studi Senesi 357-417.

Glossæ Contrariæ — *Glossæ contrariæ di Cino da Pistoia,* (1970) 38 Tijdschrift 433.

Per un profilo — *Per un profilo della personalità scientifica di Riccardo da Saliceto,* (1971) 5 Studi in onore di Edoardo Volaterra 251.

BESTA — Enrico BESTA

Riccardo — *Riccardo Malombra* (1894, Venice).

Baldo — *Baldo e la storia letteraria del diritto,* pages 18 to 111 of *L'Opera di Baldo,* q.v.

Antonio da Butrio — *Antonio da Butrio,* (1929) 3 E.I. 565.

Mincucci — *Mincucci, Antonio,* (1934) 23 E.I. 348.

Natta — *Natta, Giorgio* (1934) 24 E.I. 304.

Niccolò de' Tedeschi — *Niccolò de' Tedeschi,* (1934) 24 E.I. 767.

Pietro d'Ancarano — *Pietro d'Ancarano,* (1935) 27 E.I. 233.

CALASSO — Francesco CALASSO, *Medio Evo del Diritto* (1954).

CONRAT — Max CONRAT, *Geschichte des Quellen und Literatur des römisches Rechts* (1891, photographically reprinted 1963).

Critica del Testo — Atti del secondo Congresso internazionale della Società italiana di storia del diritto (1971).

D.B.F. — Dictionnaire de biographie française (from 1933).

D.B.I. — Dizionario biografico degli Italiani (from 1960).

D.N.B. — Dictionary of National Biography [British] (1875-1900).

DIPLOVATATIUS — Thomas DIPLOVATATIUS, *Liber de claris Jurisconsultis* (1511), edited by F. SCHULZ, H. KANTOROWICZ, and G. RABOTTI, (1968) 10 Studia Gratiana.

DOLEZALEK — Gero DOLEZALEK

die Casus Codicis — *die Casus Codicis des Wilhelmus de Cabriano,* pages 25 et seqq. of *Studien zür europäischen Rechtsgeschichte,* edited by Walter WILHELM (1972).

E.I. — *Enciclopedia Italiana* (1929-1937).

ERMINI — Giuseppe ERMINI

Castiglione — *Castiglione, Cristoforo da,* (1931) 9 E.I. 376.

Diplovataccio — *Diplovataccio, Tommaso* (1931) 12 E.I. 967.

Marsili — *Marsili, Ippolito* (1934) 22 E.I. 423.

Perugia — *Storia dell' Università di Perugia* (1971), two volumes but continuous pagination.

FEENSTRA — Robert FEENSTRA

Codi — *À propos d'un nouveau manuscrit de la version latine du Codi,* (1967) 13 Studia Gratiana 57-81.

Guido de Cumis — *Les Casus Instutionum de Guido de Cumis,* Études en souvenir de Georges Chevrier, Vol. I = (1968-69) 29 Mémoires de la société pour l'histoire du droit et des institutions des anciens pays bourguignons, comtois et romands, pages 231 to 253.

La Glose d'Accurse — *Quelques remarques sur le texte de la glose d'Accurse sur le Digeste Vieux,* (1971) 1 Critica del Testo, pages 205 to 225.

[and see MEIJERS, Études]

FOURNIER — Paul FOURNIER

Un tournant — *Un tournant de l'Histoire du droit,* (1917) R.H.D.F.E. 129.

Montlauzun — *Guillaume de Montlauzun, canoniste,* (1921) 35 Histoire littéraire de France 467.

Gu. Cu. — *Guillaume du Cun, légiste,* (1921) 35 Histoire littéraire de France 361.

Jean Faure — *Jean Faure, légiste,* (1921) 35 Histoire littéraire de France 557.

Bohic — *Henri Bohic, canoniste,* (1938) 37 Histoire littéraire de France 153.

KANTOROWICZ — Hermann KANTOROWICZ

Schriften — *Rechtshistorische Schriften* (1970), ed. Helmut COING and Gerhard IMMEL. The page numbers in this collection are given after the original references below; and references in the footnotes carry the page-numbers of *Schriften* in brackets.

Gandinus — *Albertus Gandinus und das Strafrecht der Scholastik,* Vol. I (1907), II (1926).

Digestenvulgata — *Über die Entstehung der Digestenvulgata,* (1909) 30 Z.R. 183, (1910) 31 Z.R. 14, separately reprinted with the same paragraphs (§§) but new pagination in 1910: references are to the new pagination.

Gandinustext — *Geschichte des Gandinustextes,* (1921) 42 Z.R. 1-30; (1922) 43 Z.R. 1-44.

Accursio — *Accursio e la sua biblioteca,* (1929) 2 Rivista di storia di diritto Italiano 35 to 62 and 193 to 212.

A Medieval Grammarian — *A Medieval Grammarian on the Sources of the Law,* (1937) 15 Tijdschrift 25 to 47 (*Schriften,* 93-110).

Exceptiones Petri — *Les origines françaises des Exceptiones Petri,* (1937) 16 R.H.D.F.E. (4e série) 588 to 640 (*Schriften,* 197-230).

Studies — *Studies in the Glossators of the Roman Law* (1938, with W.W. BUCKLAND), re-issued photographically with additional notes by Peter WEIMAR (1969).

Poetical Sermon — *The Poetical Sermon of a Medieval Jurist,* (1938-39) 2 Journal of the Warburg Institute 22 to 41 (*Schriften,* 111-135).

Quaestiones — *The Quaestiones Disputatae of the Glossators,* (1939) 16 Tijdschrift 1 to 67 (*Schriften,* 231-252).

An English Theologian — *An English Theologian's View of Roman Law* (with Beryl SMALLEY), (1941-43) 1 Medieval and Renaissance Studies 237 to 252 (*Schriften* 231-244).

Greek Justinian — *A Greek Justinian Constitution Quoted in the Dissensiones Dominorum,* (1945, posthumous) 3 Seminar (Annual Extraordinary Number of the Jurist) 46 to 56 (*Schriften,* 187-196).

KUTTNER — Stephan KUTTNER

Wer war — *Wer war der Dekretalist "Abbas Antiquus"?,* (1937) 26 Z.K. 471-487.

Débuts — *Les Débuts de l'école canoniste française,* (1938) 4 Studia et Documenta 193-204.

der Kardinalat — *Die Konstitutionen des ersten allgemeinen Konzils von Lyon,* (1940) 6 Studia et Documenta 70-131, Exkursus IV (pages 124-131): *der Kardinalat des Gottfried von Trani.*

Zür neuesten — *zür neuesten Glossatorenforschung,* (1940) 6 Studia et Documenta 275 (a review of KANTOROWICZ, *Studies*).

Father — *The Father of the Science of Canon Law* (1941) 1 Jurist 2.

Bernardus — *Bernardus Compostellanus Antiquus,* (1943) 1 Traditio 277.

Glossa Ordinaria — *The Glossa Ordinaria to the Gregorian Decretals* (with Beryl SMALLEY), (1945) 60 English Historical Review 97.

Anglo-Norman Canonists — (with Eleanor RATHBONE), (1949-51) 7 Traditio 279.

Graziano — *Graziano, l'uomo e l'opera,* (1953) 1 Studia Gratiana 17-29.

Johannes Andreae (Extra) — Preface to the photographic reprint of John Andrews' *Novella* on the Extravagantes (1963).

Johannes Andreae (Clem) — *The Apostillae of Johannes Andreae on the Clementines,* (1965) 1 Études d'Histoire du Droit Canonique dédiées à Gabriel Le Bras, page 195.

Liber Secretus — *Il "Liber Secretus Iuris Caesarii" dell' Università di Bologna,* a cura di Albano SORBELLI (1938, 1942), being volumes 2 and 3 of Universitatis Bononiensis Monumenta.

LIOTTA — Filippo LIOTTA

Guido da Baisio — *Appunti per una biografia del Canonista Guido da Baisio, Arcidiacono di Bologna,* (1964) 76 Studi Senesi 7-39.

Jacobus Balduini — (1964) 76 Studi Senesi 501-508, written as an article for the D.B.I., which printed one by R. ABBONDANZA instead, (1963) 5 D.B.I. 521.

Bartolomeo da Saliceto — (1964) 76 Studi Senesi 511, written as an article for the D.B.I., which printed one by G. ORLANDELLI instead, (1964) 6 D.B.I. 766.

Barbazza — *Barbazza, Andrea,* (1964) 6 D.B.I. 146.

Burgundione — (1972) 15 D.B.I. 423.

MEIJERS — Eduard Mauritz MEIJERS

Études — *Études d'Histoire du Droit,* vols III (1959) and IV (1966), edited by R. FEENSTRA and H.F.W.D. FISCHER. The page-numbers in this collection are given after the original references below; and all references are to these.

Orléans — *De Universiteit van Orleans in de XIIIe eeuw,* (1918-19) 1 Tijdschrift 108-132, 443-488, (1920-21) 2 Tijdschrift 460-518, translated into French with additions (largely by Meijers himself) and conflated with *Un Centenaire Oublié,* (1936) 14 Tijdschrift 249-266 in 3 *Études* 1-124.

Naples — Introduction to *Iuris Interpretes Saeculi XIII* (1924) (3 *Études* 149-166).

Droit international privé — *Histoire des principes fondamentaux du droit international privé à partir du moyen âge,* [1934] 3 Recueil des cours de l'Académie de droit international 543 (not reprinted in *Études*).

Sommes — *Sommes, Lectures et Commentaires,* (1934) Atti del Congresso Internazionale di diritto Romano, vol. I, pages 431 to 490 (3 Études 211-244).

Droit féodal — *Les glossateurs et le droit féodal,* (1934) 13 Tijdschrift 129-149 (3 *Études* 261-270).

Toulouse — *La première époque de ... l'université de Toulouse,* introduction (pages III to XLII) to *Responsa Doctorum Tholosanorum* (1938) (3 *Études* 167-208).

L'équité et la loi — *Le conflit entre l'équité et la loi chez les premiers glossateurs,* (1941), 17 Tijdschrift 117-135 (4 *Études* 142-156).

NAZ — *Dictionnaire de Droit canon,* edited by Robert NAZ in seven volumes (1935-1965).

L'Opera di Baldo — ed. Oscar SCALVANTI (1901).

PATETTA — Federigo PATETTA

Opere attribuite — *delle opere recentemente attribuite ad Irnerio,* (1895) 8 Bullettino dell' Istituto di Diritto Romano 39-154 (or in his collected articles, *Fonti Giuridiche Medievali* (1967), pages 341-456).

R.H.D.F.E. — Revue historique de Droit français et étranger.

RAMBAUD — Jacqueline RAMBAUD-BUHOT, *Le Legs de l'ancien droit: Gratien,* pages 49 to 129 of G. LE BRAS, Ch. LEFEBVRE and J. RAMBAUD, *L'Âge classique 1140-1378: Sources et Théorie de Droit* (1965), being Vol. VII of G. LE BRAS (ed.), *Histoire du Droit et des Institutions de l'Église en Occident.*

RASHDALL — Hastings RASHDALL, *The Universities of Europe in the Middle Ages,* 2nd edition, edited by F.M. POWICKE and A.B. EMDEN (1936).

SANTINI, *La Contessa Matilde* — Giovanne SANTINI, *La Contessa Matilde, lo "Studium," e Bologna "Città aperta" del XI secolo,* (1971) Studi Matildici (Atti e Memorie del II convegno di studi matildici, 1970), page 409.

SARTI — Mauro SARTI, *De Claris Archigymnasii Bononiensis Professoribus* (1769, 1772), re-edited 1888, 1896, and the re-edition photographically reprinted in 1962.

SAVIGNY — Friedrich Carl von SAVIGNY, *Geschichte des Römisches Rechts in Mittelalter*, 2nd edition, vols. IV, V and VI (1850), all reprinted photographically in 1961. The first edition of these volumes was translated in French by Charles GUENOUX (1839), and the second edition into Italian by Emmanuele BOLLATI (1854-1857).

SCALVANTI, *Baldo* — Oscar SCALVANTI, *Notizie e documenti sulle vite di Baldo, Angelo e Pietro degli Ubaldi*, pages 181 to 312 of *L'Opera di Baldo* (1901).

SORBELLI — Albano SORBELLI

Padova prima del 1222 — *Notizie di professori e insegnamenti in Padova prima del 1222*, (1922) 7 Studi e Memorie per la storia dell' università di Bologna, 119.

[See also *Liber Secretus*]

Studia et Documenta — Studia et Documenta Historiae Juris.

Tijdschrift — Tijdschrift voor Rechtsgeschiedenis (= Revue d'Histoire du Droit).

TORELLI — Pietro TORELLI

Scritti — *Scritti di Storia del Diritto Italiano* (1959). The page numbers in this collection are given after the original references below; and references in footnotes carry the page numbers of *Scritti* in brackets.

Documenti su Guido da Suzzara — (with E.P. VICINI), (1929) Rassegna per la storia dell' università di Modena, 63-89 (319-348).

La Codificazione e la Glossa — (1934) Atti del congresso internazionale di diritto romano (Bologna), vol. I, pages 329-343 (265-278).

Sulle orme di Guido da Suzzara — (1935) Scritti varii dedicati al prof. Eugenio Masè-Dari, pages 57 to 78 (295-315).

Nuova edizione — *Nuova edizione della glossa accursiana alle Istituzioni: risultate e speranze*, (1939-40) Rendiconti delle sessioni della regia accademia delle scienze dell' istituto di Bologna (classe di scienze morali), 4th series, Vol. III, pages 98-113 (281-292).

WEIMAR — Peter WEIMAR

Entstehung — *Zür Entstehung des Tübinger Rechtsbuch*, pages 1-24 of *Studien zür europäischen Rechtsgeschichte*, ed. Walter WILHELM (1972).

[and see KANTOROWICZ, *Studies*]

Z.K. — Zeitschrift der Savigny-Stiftung für Rechtsgeschichte, Kanonistische Abteilung.

Z.R. — Zeitschrift der Savigny-Stiftung für Rechtsgeschichte, Romanistische Abteilung.

ZONTA — G. ZONTA, *Francesco Zabarella* (1915).

Chapter I

Prologue

(500 - 1100)

The Setting of the Scene[1]

1. Bologna and Roman Law. — The story begins close to 1100 at Bologna in northern Italy, then included in the Papal States but in fact self-governing. Roman law in the form given it at Constantinople under Justinian's orders was in force in Italy by virtue of that Emperor's proclamation in A.D. 554 on its reconquest from the Ostrogoths.[2] Much of Italy fell a few years later under the yoke of new Germanic invaders, the Lombards; but much remained free of them. Ravenna on the Adriatic in the northern half of Italy was the seat of the imperial representative, whose control reached inland in this area just far enough to take in Bologna: Modena and Reggio a few miles further were Lombard.

2. Justinian. — Justinian's publications, let us remind ourselves, were labelled Institutes, Digest and Code — words which do not mean what we mean by them in legal speech today. The Institutes in four Books (about 45,000 words)[3] introduced students to the law, arranging

---

1. Most of this Chapter depends on Calasso (1954), in particular his Chapters 3, 8 and 11.
2. Roman law in its older presentation was still in force, the Ostrogoths having deliberately continued it. In southern France, untouched by Justinian's reconquest, Roman law survived in the form of the "Roman Law of the Visigoths" (later called "Alaric's Breviary"), whose sources were the earlier Code (of Theodosius II, A.D. 438), the earlier Institutes (of Gaius), and various low-grade anthologies of the juristic observations later compiled *in extenso* in Justinian's Digest.
3. This figure is a rough count, designed to give only an idea of the relative lengths of the works in question. The same is true of the other word-counts in the book. The length of an average English translation is half as many words again. As a ready standard of reference, this book has about 50,000 words of text, which would come to about the same figure in Latin if the notes were included.

the subject-matter systematically. The Digest in fifty Books (something over 700,000 words) is a compilation of extracts from the works of eminent jurisconsults, arranged also in order of subject-matter, but the order is far less logically satisfying. The Code in twelve Books (something under 400,000 words) collected in more or less the same order extracts from the pronouncements of the emperors: in the early days these had been judicial (whether by way of decision on final appeal or of directives on reference from lower judicial authorities), but by Justinian's time they were frankly legislative and included much purposive law reform. Of all these compositions only the Institutes were in unilingual Latin: the others left in Greek the many passages originally in that language. After promulgation this corpus was supplemented — and even in part superseded — by further imperial legislation which we now call the Novels. The Novels were not officially collected, and in those parts of Italy to which they could be applied two unofficial collections were known: an Epitome called Julian's, of 122 decrees or "constitutions," and the AUTHENTICUM, in which 134 "constitutions" were reproduced *in extenso*, the Greek decrees in a bad Latin translation. The Epitome rapidly drove the Authenticum out of circulation.

3. Earliest Canon Law. — The church had her own rules governing (at that time) principally her own administration, but touching also the moral duties of the faithful. Compilations were made of these too, the earliest Latin version (which has not survived) being superseded about A.D. 500 by that of a Greek-speaking monk, Dennis the Slight (*Dionysius Exiguus*). He divided his material into two parts, first the legislative rules ("canons," hence canon law) of various Councils, and secondly papal pronouncements in particular cases, whether solutions to administrative difficulties or judicial decisions: these latter were legislative only to the extent that they constituted precedents. None of this was affected by Justinian's proclamation of 554.

4. Political Geography to 1100. — Five centuries later Italy had long since ceased to be divided between Constantinople and the Lombards. At the head of the Adriatic Venice was independent, as was Genoa at the head of the Tyrrhenian Sea. The Franks under Charlemagne had conquered the Lombards in the north, and the Norman kingdom of Naples had engulfed both imperialist remnants and Lombard duchies in the south. Between the two straggled the Papal States, comprising so much of the northern half as the Lombards had not conquered: this was the Roman region on the one hand and the area between the Appenines and the Adriatic on the other, the Romagna (round Ravenna) and the march of Ancona. The two were joined by a corridor including Perugia. Under Charlemagne the Frankish dominion in the north included both the Lombard kingdom and the Papal States, and the German Emperors were the insecure successors to Charlemagne's suzerainty.

5. Law and the Schools to 1100. — These switches in mastery had at first little influence on the law, which remained Lombard in the regions which the Lombards had overrun — in the south Benevento, and in the north Lombardy proper (whose capital was Pavia) and Tuscany (with Florence, Pisa and Siena) — and remained Roman elsewhere.

Wherever Roman law ran, the Institutes and the first nine Books of the Code were known and regarded as authoritative, together with Julian's Epitome of the Novels: the last three Books of the Code, dealing with public law and no longer applicable to the changed circumstances, were forgotten, as was the whole of the Digest. The courts had never ceased to exist, and this was the law they administered at the instance of a bar whose existence was equally unbroken. The few writings which have survived to us from this period — all anonymous — were perhaps the work of practitioners in their spare time; for there is no sign of a law-school (despite later assertions) at Rome after the sixth century or at Ravenna at any time. At Ravenna however there were lawyers whose opinions, singly or together, had a degree of authority: they were sufficiently homogeneous to be called a "school" of thought.

Romanist principles gained sufficient prestige to provide, by the end of the millennium, the spectacles through which Lombard law was regarded: the *language* of all Germanic law from the time when it was first reduced to writing had been Latin, however desperately barbarised; and by 1100 it was no longer barbaric. A tradition of study of and comment upon the Lombard law-books seems to have centred on Pavia, the ancient Lombard capital; but at Pavia too there is no indication of anything like a school in the sense of an institution in which law was taught as such.

Taught however it was, as illustrative of the three literary subjects — grammar, logic and rhetoric — which made up the medieval "trivium" and which preceded the more mathematical "quadrivium." It is of some importance that law entered into the first part of the degree course, for a high proportion of students got no further. Students who completed both parts earned the title of Master of Arts and could then teach. The schools which dispensed these courses were from the dark ages ecclesiastical: all the teachers and most of the students were clerics. In Italy however these ages never reached the degree of darkness which engulfed Europe beyond the Alps: one did not need to seek refuge in the Church in order to think. Lay schools therefore existed, and for some time before 1100 that at Bologna had had a wide reputation. Such a school, church or lay, was called a *studium*; and a *studium* which attained to the dignity reserved by us for a University was later popularly styled a *Studium Generale.*

6. Canon Law to 1100. — By 1100 the field governed by canon law had taken in much that to our eyes is temporal. On the ground that moral duties were involved, it was the courts of the church that decided litigation in respect of marriage, wills, and often of contracts, as well as disputes of any nature where a churchman was defendant. Such disputes were decided according to the principles of Roman law, but subject to moral modification, and these principles so modified counted now as part of canon law. Canon law was no more a subject of self-contained instruction than was civil law; but it entered into the theological syllabus which succeeded a Master's degree.

Unlike the Roman law applied by the temporal courts, canon law had not ceased to develop by legislation. Canons continued to be adopted by Councils, and Popes continued to give decisions, even to legislate directly. Dennis' compilation had therefore long been superseded, the two most noteworthy recent collections being those of Burkhardt of Worms at the beginning of the eleventh century and of Ivo of Chartres in its last decade. Ivo included apposite excerpts from Justinian's compilations, even (at last) from the Digest.

7. Pope and Emperor to 1100. — To the merely political conflict inherent in the later Emperors' claim to have succeeded Charlemagne in his suzerainty over the agitated cities of the old Lombard kingdom on the one hand, and over the Papal States on the other, was gradually added the papal claim to ultimate superiority (under God) over every earthly ruler, including the Emperor. From this elemental clash was struck the spark to rekindle the quenched torch of learned and speculative law.

8. The Recovery of the Digest. — For if the Institutes and the Code were still familiar, the very existence of the Digest can confidently be said to have been still unknown in the 60s of the eleventh century;[4] but it was equally certainly known in 1076, when it was inappositely cited in a judgment rendered in Tuscany.[5] As this is just the time when searchers commissioned by Hildebrand (Pope Gregory VII from 1073 to 1085, but the driving force in papal politics long before then) were combing the libraries of Italy for legal ammunition in his bitter controversy with the Emperor over the investitures, it may be supposed that it was turned up by them.[6] It is certain that these searchers discovered and reinstated the Authenticum,[7] and from the Digest itself about a hundred excerpts made their way into a canon-law collection made at Rome[8] which in turn was among Ivo's sources. It is to be remarked that these excerpts represent a text which is not that of the only ancient manuscript now surviving, written in southern Italy in the second half of the sixth century[9] and located at least by the 12th century in Pisa.[10] They represent another (lost) text, conventionally styled "Codex S[ecundus]", which was the ancestor of all copies later made in the Bologna school. These two texts were later distinguished at Bologna as the *Littera Bononiensis* or *Vulgata*, and the *Littera Pisana*: the latter is now usually called the *Florentina*, because Florence took this celebrated antiquity from Pisa in 1406 as spoils of war (paragraph 133 below), and has possessed it ever since.

But knowledge of the existence of the Digest, in whatever text, did not mean that anyone had read it with sufficient attention[11] to realise its possibilities as a mine of juristic thought, rich in the subtle discussion and distinction which makes of the law an intellectual discipline.

9. Bologna to 1100. — Apart from knowledge of the Digest, legal reform was afoot in Bologna in the last half of the eleventh century.

---

4. KANTOROWICZ, *Digestenvulgata* (1910), §. 5, at page 20.
5. Printed at 4 FICKER, *Forschungen zur Reichs - und Rechtsgeschichte Italiens* (1874), n. 73, pages 99 and following; quoted at 1 RASHDALL 112, and (with a misprint) by CALASSO, page 506.
6. FOURNIER, *Un Tournant* (1917), at page 152.
7. FOURNIER, *loc. cit.*, at page 150.
8. They are already in the *Britannica* (so called because it is in the British Museum) — CONRAT (1891), page 353, note 3. And it was probably not the *Britannica* itself that was Ivo's source, but an earlier compilation from which the *Britannica* was also derived: see FOURNIER, *Un tournant* (1917), at pages 145, 146, 152.
9. KANTOROWICZ, *Digestenvulgata*, §. 4, pages 12 to 19.
10. KANTOROWICZ, *op. cit.*, §. 5, page 21.
11. The celebrated judgment of 1076 which cites the Digest wholly misunderstands the passage to which it seems to refer: KANTOROWICZ, *An English Theologian* (1943), at page 241 (234). And Petrus Crassus of Ravenna in 1084 cites as from the Digest a passage which is in fact in the Code: FOURNIER, *Un tournant* (1917), at page 153.

In particular new ideas of notarial drafting centred on the palace of the "orthodox" bishop.[12] For Bologna from 1078 to 1104[13] was in the peculiar position of having two rival bishops, one now reckoned as "orthodox" being faithful to Rome, and the other "schismatic" and supporting the Emperor against the Pope. Legal experts (*jurisperiti*) sat as assessors in the courts, and were styled *legis doctor*, though this term had no implication either of a law degree or of law teaching: one such is mentioned as early as 1063.[14]

Politically the most important personage in northern Italy was the anti-imperial Countess Matilda, who succeeded in 1076 to the government of dominions including part of Lombardy and the whole of Tuscany. They did not include Bologna, but as early as 1079-80[15] she was supporting the "orthodox" bishop; and in her courts Bolognese *legis doctores* increasingly replaced those from staunchly imperialist Ravenna.

---

12. SANTINI, *La Contessa Matilde* (1971), at pages 412, 417, 418.
13. SANTINI, *loc. cit.*, at page 410.
14. Stephanus of Ferrara, SANTINI, *loc. cit.*, at page 417; Albertus of Bologna, in 1067, *ibid.*, page 421; Iginulfus of Bologna, *legis doctor et judex aule regie*, 1076, 1085, *ibid.*, page 413.
15. SANTINI, *loc. cit.*, page 412.

CHAPTER II

First Steps

(1100 - 1600)

TEXT, GLOSS, TREATISE

10. Peppo and Irnerius. — The first to teach Roman law as such appears to have been PEPPONE (*Peppo*) — the name is a common diminutive of Giuseppe or Joseph.[1] He left nothing in writing; we have no idea of the extent of his learning; and we cannot even be sure that the scene of his teaching was BOLOGNA. It is however certain that he was in some sense the precursor[2] of a Bolognese Master of Arts named WARNER (*Warnerius, Guarnerius*), "or, as he was called later on, IRNERIUS."[3] It would perhaps seem pedantic in the following lines not to use the latter familiar form; but we must not lose sight of plain Mr Warner behind this fancy dress[4] which he himself saw no need to assume.

---

1. The earliest spelling was "Peppo," not "Pepo." This was a common name both in Tuscany and the Romagna, and the two documents of 1076 and after 1078, usually thought to refer to him, may very well concern another person of the same name. The scanty evidence was authoritatively dissected by KANTOROWICZ just before his death in *An English Theologian* (1943).
2. Ralph BLACK (*Radulfus Niger*), *Moralia Regum* (written just before 1189, but probably in this respect a reminiscence from student days at Paris before 1170): "Master Peppone was the rising dawn of the reborn beginnings of civil law, which Master Warner thereafter propagated" — KANTOROWICZ, *An English Theologian,* at page 250 (242).
3. KANTOROWICZ, *Studies,* at page 33.
4. The contemporary latinisation was *Warnerius* in nearly all the documents printed at 4 SAVIGNY, pages 12 and 13. Of the literary sources, Ralph Black (note 2 above) has the same form, but more commonly it was *Guarnerius.* He signed "*Wernerius,*" which gives the modern German Werner, and *Gwernerius* is also found. The earliest deformation was *Yrnerius*: could this be due to a misunderstanding of a purely scribal confusion between the letters .g. (his siglum, paragraph 22 below) and .y.? The suggestion was made by PATETTA, *Opere Attribuite* (1895), at page 150 (452), and stranger things have happened.

11. Irnerius: the Texts. — "Irnerius" had not studied under Peppone or anyone else: he taught himself.[5] And if it can no longer be said that he discovered the existence of the Digest, it was he who first drank deep and worshipped at this Pierian spring. Perhaps at the prompting of the Countess Matilda[6] — though one is at a loss to divine why she should have been interested[7] — he seems to have begun in the early 1090's[8] to write out his own copy of the lost "Codex S," improving its mistaken readings as best he could by comparison with parallel passages, or even by inspired guessing[9] — an exercise in textual criticism which had no precedent, and which was to be the distinguishing mark of the school which he founded. Of the numerous passages in Greek, those in Book 29 seem to have been already in a Latin translation in "Codex S:" the rest were either omitted or still in Greek. Whichever it was, Irnerius did not know them.

With the first nine Books of the Code he dealt more radically, interpolating[10] extracts from the newly discovered Authenticum at the points where they would have been included if the Code had been compiled after instead of before their issue. He remained in ignorance

---

5. Odofred (died 1265, paragraph 65 below), quoted by KANTOROWICZ, *An English Theologian,* at page 238 (232).
6. According to a chronicle of the next century: *dominus Wernerius libros legum, qui dudum neglecti fuerant nec quisquam in eis studuerat, ad petitionem Mathildæ comitissæ renovavit.*
   It seems to be accepted that this entry has a nearly contemporary origin; but the precise connotation of *petitio* has aroused fierce controversy. A recent suggestion is that it arises from a misunderstanding of a dedication to this formidable lady of a set of volumes of Justinian's texts: G. ARNALDI, *Qualche osservazioni sulle origini "spontanee" dell' Università di Bologna,* (1970) 8 Cultura 572, at page 580.
7. At 1 RASHDALL 116 is the suggestion that she hoped to establish an anti-imperial counterweight to the imperialistic lawyers of Ravenna. He seems to have been thinking of an instigation by Matilda to found a law-school rather than to restore the law-books; but from any point of view such an objective would have been a grievous miscalculation. As we shall see later, no one could have been more imperialist than Irnerius himself and the Bologna doctors after him. The guess that Matilda "wanted to counterbalance the influence of the Imperialist school [sic] at Ravenna by establishing a centre of studies in Roman law that would act on the Papal side" is repeated as fact by Sir Paul VINOGRADOFF, *Roman Law in Medieval Europe* (ed. 1929) at page 55. He continues with the pure fiction that she sent him to Rome to study law first, and that his school at Bologna started about 1088. All this is part of the *somnia Fittingiana* (H. FITTING's dream-world) denounced first by MOMMSEN, and methodically demolished by KANTOROWICZ: a citation of the latter's *Studies* (1938) at page 225 must suffice.
8. KANTOROWICZ, *Digestenvulgata,* §. 18, at page 90.
9. KANTOROWICZ, *Digestenvulgata,* §§. 11, 12 and 13, at pages 40 to 61. The author of all these operations is identified as Irnerius in §§. 17 to 21, pages 88 to 117.
10. 4 SAVIGNY, pages 42 and following.

of the Greek passages in the Code as much as of those in the Digest, and (since he did not interpolate them at all) of the whole of the last three Books: he also makes no reference to these Books in his cross-references (below). Of the Authenticum itself he considered only 97 of its 134 "constitutions" worth including in his canon. The Institutes of courses formed part of his material.

12. Arrangement of the Texts. — Irnerius found the Books of the Institutes, Digest and Code already numbered (but not named) and divided into Titles (or chapters as we should say in ordinary English) both numbered and named. Each Title of the Digest and Code consists of a series of extracts not then numbered or named: we identify them by a serial number as we do the Titles, but Irnerius cited them by their first words, with the name of the Title of which they formed part. Each extract was referred to as a "law" (*lex*) whether its source was legislative or juristic; but the interpolations in the Code from the Authenticum were distinguished as "authentics." The 97 "constitutions" selected from the Authenticum itself were grouped not in Books or Titles but in nine "Collations."

The whole of the Irnerian canon, or *Corpus Juris Civilis* as it was later called, was divided into five volumes, an arrangement which was unaffected by the invention of printing and continued until quite recently. The first three volumes were the Digest; the fourth the first nine Books of the Code; and the fifth or Small Volume (*Parvum Volumen*) contained the Institutes, the Authenticum and (later) the last Three Books (*Tres Libri*) of the Code, which thus remained separated from the first nine till long after the Renaissance.

Another important addition which had to wait more than a generation after Irnerius was the translation of the Greek passages which he had had to omit. This was done for the Digest by BURGUNDIO of PISA (c. 1110-1193) from the *Littera Pisana* in his home town.[11] But no translation of the Greek constitutions in the Code was accepted into the Bolognese canon throughout the middle ages: some old manuscripts carried them in Greek, but the Bologna canon left blanks till humanistic research at the Renaissance filled them. Some private translations existed: the Catalan PETER of CARDONA[12] is credited with abbreviated

11. 4 SAVIGNY, pages 394 and 398, citing Odofred. Burgundio made other translations from Greek; and his knowledge of that language led to his being sent on two embassies to Constantinople in 1138 and 1171 — pages 398 and 399. Compare LIOTTA, *Burgundione* (1972).

12. KANTOROWICZ, *Greek Justinian* (1945), 54-56 (194-196); WEIMAR, *Entstehung* (1972), page 18, citing (at note 93) earlier discussion.

Latin versions of at least five (at least one known to Bulgarus, below), made probably between 1155 and 1162 when he was teaching law in Southern France. From 1166 to 1174 Peter was in Rome as cardinal.

The three volumes devoted to the Digest divide its bulk unequally (350, 278 and 292 pages in Mommsen's text), and the points chosen for division make no sense. Nor is it apparent why the three volumes were called respectively the OLD DIGEST, the INFORTIATUM and the NEW DIGEST. The tradition is that Irnerius "discovered" the Digest in bits, the Infortiatum last, and therefore constituting a "reinforcement" of the work by the insertion of its missing middle. The "tradition" is no more than a guess, and there is a difficulty: *infortiatum* could mean "reinforced," but hardly "reinforcement." There is no accepted explanation of this conundrum; but it is a plausible suggestion that "Codex S" was already in three segments or volumes, the division being intentional but irrational, except to the uninstructed caprice of the earlier scribe or of a predecessor:[13] there is no such division of the "Littera Pisana." The names are likely to be student slang of the first generation, the New Digest because it starts with the Title *de Operis Novi Nunciatione*; the Old Digest by contrast, and by analogy with the Old and New Testaments; and the Infortiatum because it was "imprisoned" between them — an acceptable medieval meaning of the word.[14]

13. Irnerius' Career. — It must have cost Irnerius many "painful" years to constitute his text, not only copying and emending but "glossing" by adding cross-references in the margins and verbal explanations between the lines. He was not a churchman and had therefore no benefice: we do not know certainly how he won his bread while he was so occupied, or even before. He is said to have been a teacher of "arts;" and there is some reason — but not much — for supposing him to have been a notary. He was however in the succession of the *jurisperiti*, appearing several times at the beginning of the twelfth century as an assessor to judgments, and was evidently of some civic

13. KANTOROWICZ, *Digestenvulgata*, §. 25, pages 135 to 138 as confirmed in *A Medieval Grammarian* at pages 39 (104) and following. He suggests that the first split, after Title XXIV.ii on Divorce, is due to divorce meaning "split;" while the second, before Title XXXIX.i, *de Operis Novi Nunciatione*, is a misunderstanding of this heading as an "Announcement (sc. by the Emperor) of a New Work." The Old and New Digest were themselves (later) divided into two parts each for the purposes of instruction, and the Infortiatum into three, of which the third was called the *Tres Partes*: nothing hangs on this. The Code and the Institutes were also divided into two parts each for the same purpose: the first part of the Institutes ran to III.xii, and the second part from III.xiv to the end — FEENSTRA, *Guido de Cumis* (1968-69), at page 243.
14. KANTOROWICZ, *Digestenvulgata*, §. 29, at pages 147 to 150.

importance at this time. When the German Emperor Henry V descended on Italy to garner the territories of the Countess Matilda, gathered without heirs to her fathers in 1115, it was Irnerius who met him in 1116 to excuse Bologna for its anti-imperial excesses at the moment of her death.[15] In 1118 he was at Rome taking a prominent part in the election of an anti-pope in the imperial interest,[16] and for this he was excommunicated by name,[17] apparently till 1122.[18] He may have lived to about 1130.[19]

14. Irnerius the Teacher. — In all this there is no mention of teaching. If we accept the unanimous tradition of succeeding generations that Irnerius founded the law-school at Bologna by starting to teach Justinian's law there,[20] it must have been a small affair at first.[21] There is nothing like the excitement at Paris at the meteoric career of his contemporary Abelard, the first defiantly critical theologian — in fact no contemporary notice even of the existence of a law-school. And no one is claimed to have received instruction from Irnerius' own lips except the "Four Doctors" who are about to engage us. Was it then a mere study group? In the existing state of the evidence this is perhaps the most likely guess. Whatever the size of the audience may have been, 1100 is a probable date for the commencement of his teaching.[22]

---

15. SANTINI, *La Contessa Matilde* (1971), at page 411.
16. "*Magister Guarnerius de Bononia et plures legis periti:*" Chronicle of LANDOLFO di SAN PAOLO, quoted at 1 RASHDALL, page 119.
17. "*Guarnerius Bononiensis legis peritus,*" at the Council of Reims in October 1119. No list of the names of those excommunicated appears in any of the printed records of this Council, but there is a list in a twelfth-century manuscript at St. John's College, Oxford, reported in 1933 and revealed to legal historians by G. de VERGOTTINI, *Lo Studio di Bologna,* (1956) 1 Studi e Memorie per la Storia dell' Università di Bologna (new series), 19, at page 33.
18. All such excommunications were lifted by the Concordat of Worms: G. CENCETTI, *Studium fuit Bononie,* (1966) 7 Studi Medievali (third series), 781, at page 802.
19. KANTOROWICZ, *Digestenvulgata,* §. 18, at page 90, and *Studies,* at page 69.
20. According to Odofred, "*Dominus Yrnerius ... fuit ... primus qui docuit in civitate ista; nam primo cepit studium esse in civitate ista in artibus, et ... Dominus Yrnerius, dum doceret in artibus in civitate ista, cum fuerunt deportati libri legales, cepit per se studere in libris nostris, et studendo cepit docere in legibus, et ipse fuit maximi nominis, et fuit primus illuminator scientie nostre ...*" Whatever the chronicler may have meant by the *petitio* of the Countess Matilda, he was not referring to the *teaching* of Irenerius, so that the voluminous discussion on whether Matilda had jurisdiction to authorise teaching at Bologna is all beside the point.
21. M. ASCHERI (reviewing E. SPAGNESI, *Wernerius Bononiensis Judex*), (1970) 82 Studi Senesi 302, at page 309.
22. His own students were operating not much later: KANTOROWICZ, *Digestenvulgata,* §. 18, at page 91; *Studies,* page 69.

Teaching probably required from the begining, as it always had for subjects earlier taught, a licence from the ecclesiastical authorities, in this case the Archdeacon of Bologna.[23] The teacher's title was still "Master" in the time of Irnerius,[24] and in the next generation also for all but the "Four Doctors:" after them "Doctor" was the usual title for a law teacher in Italy.

15. The Four Doctors. — The "Four Doctors" were BULGARUS (so latinised: I do not know what it means) BULGARINI; MARTIN GOSIA; HUGH (*Ugo*) of the RAVENNA GATE (in Bologna); and JAMES (*Jacobus*) without surname. That they taught, and to classes of students, is attested by several pieces of evidence, first an anecdote which shows that the class-room was not so very different from what it is eight centuries later. This was the roar of laughter[25] that greeted a remark by Bulgarus the day after his marriage to a widow. He began his lecture as usual by reading the "law" on which he proposed to comment, and the "law" began: "It is no untouched field that we are entering."

An extension of classroom instruction, certainly started in this generation, was the moot court at which a Doctor presided over arguments between students on problems arising in the circumstances of the times, and to which the solution was not to be found directly in the texts: the doctor set the problem, and after the argument gave judgment. The style of argumentation almost certainly reflected contemporary court-room practice; but the technical terms for each step in the proceedings come from Justinian. The proceedings are reported (by students) under the name of *Questiones Disputate,*[26] to be distinguished from the *Questiones Dominorum,* or more usually *Dissensiones Dominorum,* meaning succinct accounts of the differences between the masters themselves.[27] Most of the "disputations" reported had taken place before Bulgarus, and most of the "dissensions" were those between Bulgarus and Martin.

16. Strict Law and Equity. — These two typified two tendencies which have always divided lawyers and always will. Bulgarus was

---

23. 1 RASHDALL 231, 232 (his editors).
24. E.g. notes 2 and 16 above.
25. Standard Gloss (by Accursius, paragraph 59 below) on Code III.i.14 (*rem non novam aggredimur*). RASHDALL in 6 *Cambridge Medieval History* 559, at page 582, cites as an example of student tyranny the regulation that a professor may take a day off to get married, but no honeymoon: it would be interesting to know how frequent honeymoons were at the time.
26. KANTOROWICZ, *Studies,* pages 81 to 85; and *Quæstiones* (1939), pages 5 (140), 21 (151-2), 35 (161-2) and following, 52 to 59 (174-179).
27. KANTOROWICZ, *Studies,* page 87.

content — indeed proud, as had been Irnerius — to know the law, to understand it, to explain away apparent discrepancies. Martin was not content: he criticised. And when a text was in conflict not merely with another text but with his idea of justice, he did not explain it away but said it was wrong:[28] this earned him the reputation of the champion of "equity." It is easy and customary to exaggerate these differences — not even Martin could find much that was inequitable in Roman law — but they must not divert us from what these early teachers had in common: their enormous erudition, and a familiarity with and understanding of the often extremely difficult texts they were expounding, which has rarely been rivalled since and is certainly not rivalled today.

17. Influence on Practice. — The subject taught was Justinian's law in its pure state. For the whole of the twelfth century the law-school studiously ignored the existence of contemporary practice, except in the disputations. But contemporary practice certainly did not ignore the school: it was the Chancellor of the papal court at Rome who specifically asked Bulgarus (between 1125 and 1141)[29] for his treatise on civil procedure according to Justinian (paragraph 25 below) because it was considered to be much superior to the custom of the time. The prestige of the law-school was probably behind the rapid conversion at this time of the cities of Tuscany from Lombard to Roman law;[30] and in 1162 Hugh, with the title of imperial judge,[31] was assessor in a great cause at Siena, framing the judgment with the clarity and in the terminology which Bologna taught.[32]

18. Studium and Universitas. — By this generation then it is clear that the law-school at Bologna had become an institution, and that law had taken its place alongside theology and medicine (established at Salerno since at least A.D. 1000[33]) as a subject of higher education.

---

28. More precisely, while both agreed that "equity" prevailed over the strict law, for Bulgarus this meant equity as discoverable in the law, what we should call the "intention of the legislator;" while Martin meant the principles of justice, even if nowhere legislated, what the canonists were to call later "natural law" — MEIJERS, *L'équité et la loi* (1941). Compare also KANTOROWICZ, *Studies*, at pages 87, 88 and 91.
29. KANTOROWICZ, *Studies*, pages 69 and 71.
30. Specific dates are 1161 for Pisa, 1176 for Siena, Roman law having in both cases "long" been the rule. Arrigo SOLMI, *Ugo di Porta Ravennate*, (1908), I.ii. Studi e Memorie per la Storia dell' Università di Bologna, 101-115, considers 1151 the probable date for the instruction by the Emperor Conrad (III not I) to the judges at Rome to apply nothing but Roman law.
31. *Ugo Bononiensis de Porta Ravennate gloriosissimi imperatoris Friderigi judex.*
32. SOLMI, *loc. cit.*
33. I RASHDALL 78.

It is perhaps still too early to say that students flocked to Bologna from all over Europe; but there were certainly many from outside Bologna, and it seems that there was already a demand for copies of legal texts for hire. They were hired out by "stationers;" and the control of these "stationers,"[34] as also of lodgings,[35] was among the more important functions of the student organisations which must have grown up well before the end of the century. These organisations were the only means by which the majority of students, being rightless foreigners,[36] could find protection against the local authorities: their weapon was the economic advantage which the local community derived from their presence.[37] It was this student organisation that the word *Universitas* first described; and it was this numerous concentration of students that was the earliest to suggest to us a parallel with our own Universities.[38]

19. Juristic Prestige. — It was again some time before those learned in the law would find themselves at the receiving end of the comfortable illusion — like psychologists in our day — that they were indispensable to society and to the state. But there is a statute of Bologna dated to 1158 providing that no one might be judge or consultant without having studied law for five years[39] — how different from the later common-law criterion of so many year's practice at the bar. And there is the "constitution" of the German Emperor Frederick I (Barbarossa), promulgated in the same year (1158) at the Diet of Roncaglia, and protecting law-students away from home: Bologna is not specifically mentioned, but no claim to a law-school is made for anywhere else at this date.

20. Juristic Imperialism. — This Emperor had reason to be grateful to the Four Doctors who, at this same Diet, advised him that with the title of Emperor he had inherited the absolute supremacy in law of his Roman predecessors. The text of the constitution protecting students emphasises this identity of sovereignty by directing (presumably on the advice of the Doctors) its insertion in Justinian's Code, in the Title

34. Including the accuracy of their copies — *op. cit.* pages 189, 190. It is unfortunate that the same meticulous control was not exercised over the Renaissance printed editions.
35. Including rents — *op. cit.* page 191.
36. *Op. cit.,* pages 157 to 159.
37. *Op. cit.,* page 165.
38. Bologna had an independent faculty of arts, including from 1260 or so medicine as an upper tier, and from 1364 a faculty of theology; but these were of small significance beside the faculty of law: 1 RASHDALL 233 to 253.
39. *Op. cit.,* at page 259.

Ne Filius pro Patre (or IV.xiii as we describe it) in the same way as Irnerius had inserted Justinian's Novels.[40] That legal theory did not correspond with political reality was however demonstrated after twenty-five years of struggle by the Peace of Constance (1183), when Frederick I acknowledged his defeat by the Lombard cities and their consequent independence. Legal theory accounted for this by calling it a voluntary delegation of authority.[41]

21. The End of the Generation. — Bulgarus and Martin hardly survived Roncaglia.[42] Hugh and James were younger, and had probably studied under the first two as well as under Irnerius: James died last in 1178, so that none was left by the Peace of Constance. These two left little visible trace on the development of the law, but more than their contemporary Master ALDRIC,[43] though a few of his views were recorded and were influential.

22. Gloss and Distinction. — Apart from their oral teaching, and the recording (by others) of their judgments in moot court and of their disagreements, the Doctors also left remarks in writing, mostly GLOSSES, or what we should call footnotes to the Roman texts, were it not that they were written in all the space left vacant by the text, at the head and at the side as well as at the foot of the page. The authorship of a gloss is indicated by an initial or two at the end between full stops: Irnerius for example appears as .g. or (perhaps a scribal error) .y. It is thought that these glosses were notes by the lecturer to assist his memory, and that taken together they formed a connected (if jejune) commentary;[44] but the innumerable glosses of this generation surviving in 12th century manuscripts were at least sometimes notes by students listening to oral lectures.

Most glosses were very brief, hardly more than cross-references to other texts consonant and dissonant: there was nothing new as a literary genre in this kind of glossing. Where our "glossators" innovated was in their meticulous attention to the text itself, and on the occasions where their glosses lengthened out and included (for example) DISTINCTIONS, meaning the splitting up of concepts so that different

---

40. Another of his "constitutions" was similarly inserted; and later on a long "constitution" of his grandson Frederick II, dated 1220, was chopped up and distributed into several "authentics," like any other Novel.
41. Standard Gloss (by Accursius, paragraph 59 below) on Authenticum III.ii, §. 2 (*jusjurandum*).
42. KANTOROWICZ, *Studies*, pages 68 and 86.
43. He is mentioned from 1154 to 1172 — 4 SAVIGNY, pages 231 and following.
44. KANTOROWICZ, *Studies*, page 33.

rules applied on either side of the line drawn. In more homely language it is the sort of remark that begins with: "It makes a difference whether..."

23. Exordium and Materia. — A special opportunity for semi-independent glosses was given by the headings or "rubrics" of Titles, and in particular the name and opening words of the Institutes and of the Code. The glosses of Irnerius himself at the beginning of the Institutes were collected to constitute an introductory essay (*exordium*) in 195 words on the definition of justice and of jurisprudence, and from his glosses on the beginning of the Code to make up a similar introduction (380 words) on the definition of law, on the sources of law (its "raw material," hence *materia* for the whole of such an essay in the next generation), and on the purposes of the legislator. These two together were the cradle of what we now call general jurisprudence.[45] Bulgarus and Martin had similar essays on both Institutes[46] and Code.[47]

24. Apparatus and Lectura. — A collection of glosses on a component of the Corpus, or even on a single Title, written in the order of the text but without the text, was called an APPARATUS: one by Martin on the Institutes has been recently discovered,[48] and others by him on the Old and on the New Digest even more recently.[49] One by Bulgarus on the last Title of the Digest has long been known.[50]

The LECTURA in the sense of notes taken by a student of the lectures as given by the professor, was commoner later (and a Commentary, written by the professor himself, is not yet known at all); but in this generation a Lectura on the Institutes from Martin's lips is known. It is now seen to reproduce most of his Apparatus, but with the occasional addition that he changed his mind later.[51] Bulgarus'

---

45. *Op. cit.,* page 38. That of Irnerius on the Institutes is discussed at pages 59 to 65, and on the Code at pages 46 to 50.
46. *Op. cit.,* pages 65 to 67 (Bulgarus) and 53 (Martin).
47. *Op. cit.,* pages 42 to 46 (Bulgarus): Martin's (at page 43) was a gloss on the word "Code," but did not amount to a "materia."
48. By Meijers: KANTOROWICZ, *Studies,* at page 87.
49. On two Books of the New Digest by DOLEZALEK, (1967) 84 Z.R. 245-349: cf. WEIMAR, editing the reprint of Kantorowicz's *Studies* (1969), at page 335. On the Old Digest by WEIMAR, *Entstehung* (1972).
50. KANTOROWICZ, *Studies,* at page 69.
51. MEIJERS, *Sommes* (1934), at pages 212 to 216 of 3 *Etudes.* This has been printed as a set of glosses to the Vienna Summa (paragraph 32 below): KANTOROWICZ, *Studies,* page 87, note 12, agrees that it is not that, but does not agree that it constitutes a *lectura.*

lectures on the first nine Books of the Code were not very competently commemorated by his student WILLIAM di CABRIANO of Brescia[52] in his inappositely named *Casus Codicis* (about 45,000 words) — inappositely because *casus* naturally means a "case" or illustration, and did in fact have this meaning for later generations.[53] This work is valuable as showing that from these early times a lecturer did not go through his text minutely, but selected certain passages only as foundation for his remarks.[54] William may have been the same man as later rose to be Archbishop of Ravenna, from 1190 to his death in 1201.

25. Summula and Treatise. — A comprehensive commentary on the subject of a whole Title, not only not attached to any particular "law" in it but also gathering in what was laid down elsewhere in the Corpus on the same subject, was a Summa — or later SUMMULA, when "summa" was used (as we shall see in the next chapter) to indicate such a comment on a whole member of the Corpus. Summule are known of Bulgarus,[55] Martin,[56] and even Hugh.[57]

Comments on particular subjects, wholly independent of any particular text, even a Title, were less common: they were later called TREATISES (*Tractatus*).[58] Martin's on the law of dowry (*de Jure Dotium*)[59] (nearly 4500 words) might equally well be called a summula on the same Title of the Code, itself in the form of a treatise; but Bulgarus treatise on Civil Procedure (*Ordo Judiciorum*)[60] (less than 3000 words) has no such point of attachment.

The emergence of the Summula and of the Treatise marks a crucial turning point in the history of the law. "Pure" Roman law, as the glossators received it, resembled the common law in being a mass of solutions to particular cases, ill coordinated if coordinated at all: co-

---

52. KANTOROWICZ, *Studies*, pages 206 to 212, must now be read subject to DOLEZALEK, *die Casus Codicis* (1972), announcing discovery of two complete manuscripts of this work so far known only in fragments. For the date Dolezalek says cautiously before the end of 1158; but the middle of 1157 is mentioned near the end of the work.
53. Odofred complains more than once that this work is not really *casus* but a commentary.
54. DOLEZALEK, *die Casus Codicis*, at page 37.
55. KANTOROWICZ, *Studies*, pages 73 to 80.
56. *Op. cit.*, pages 88 to 91.
57. *Op. cit.*, pages 107 to 111.
58. On the glossators' own terminology see KUTTNER, *zür neuesten* (1940), at pages 284 and following.
59. KANTOROWICZ, *Studies*, pages 94 to 102.
60. *Op. cit.*, pages 70 to 72.

ordination began to be supplied by the three generations after Irnerius. This was however only the first step in the direction of systematisation; and before pursuing it we must look at two examples of another method, the re-arrangement of the basic texts themselves.

26. Vacarius. — The Lombard VACARIUS[61] had, like Aldric, no title but Master.[62] He must have studied at Bologna, for in his glosses he often refers to Bulgarus[63] and to Martin — usually disagreeing with the former and following the latter — and it is hardly likely that he acquired knowledge of their views elsewhere. Having been brought to England for use in a campaign of ecclesiastical politics, he set up as a teacher, fairly certainly at Oxford; and in 1149 published what he called The Poor Men's Book (*Liber Pauperum*). He took orders between 1150 and 1161,[64] and was still alive (in England) in 1198.[65]

His book was so called because his students, unable to hire texts as at Bologna, or to afford the purchase of the full texts, needed a compendium. It took the form of a series of extracts from the Corpus, arranged in nine Books[66] which corresponded fairly closely to the first nine Books of the Code, but with the addition of the tenth and eleventh Books to the first on the ground that they also dealt with public law: he was the first to make use of these Books. Relevant extracts from the Digest were present in more or less equal bulk, and where the Code was silent the Digest took over. By the order in which the extracts were placed Vacarius contrived with skill and understanding to systematise the whole. He also glossed[67] his compilation very liberally, and some of the views he expressed reached Bologna. His book continued to be the basis of study at Oxford till early in the next century, when it was superseded briefly by the fashion for the Roman texts entire.

Besides this conflation of Digest and Code, Vacarius was author of a *lectura* on the Institutes, whose influence has yet to be assessed.[68]

61. F. de ZULUETA, *Liber Pauperum,* (1927) 44 Selden Society.
62. *Op. cit.,* page xx.
63. *Op. cit.,* page cxlviii.
64. *Op. cit.,* page xvi.
65. *Op. cit.,* page xxi.
66. *Op. cit.,* pages xliv to li.
67. *Op. cit.,* pages lxviii to lxxii.
68. An edition is being prepared for the Selden Society by Peter STEIN. Meanwhile certain peculiarities in Bracton have been traced to it — J. L. BARTON, *Roman Law in England,* (1971) *Ius Romanum Medii Aevi* V. 13a, page 15, note 28.

27. Gratian. — As early as 1140,[69] that is nearly twenty years before Roncaglia, the sustained enthusiasm of the law-school engendered a by-product: this was a new compilation at Bologna of the sources of canon law by a Camaldolese monk called GRATIAN.[70] Like Aldric and Vacarius he is qualified as Master, not Doctor, and hardly anything else is known of him: if he taught the classroom was certainly not his principal work. He is last mentioned (as a judicial assessor) in 1143, and must have died then or very soon after.

The texts which he compiled were those already recognised as authoritative — extracts from canons of every kind of council, opinions of the early fathers, pronouncements of the Popes, so that in this respect his work was parallel to the Digest and Code together in civil law. There is however no evidence that Vacarius, when he put the Digest and the Code together, was influenced by Gratian's work. Textually, nearly all the extracts so compiled can be traced to one or other of the three compilations by Ivo of Chartres (paragraph 6 above).[71]

28. Arrangement of the Decreta. — But Gratian was much more than a compiler. Not only was he the first to arrange his extracts in systematic order — as Irnerius was unable to do because Justinian had already done it with authority — but he provided them with comment (*dicta*) prefaced to groups of texts and interspersed among them: he did not cast his remarks, as Vacarius was to do, in the form of glosses separate from the text. This integration of source with comment is a technique which had no parallel before or after till the case-book of our own days.

Under the influence of the dialectical method which had earned such popularity from Abelard's sensational mastery of it — but with a calmness and thoroughness of treatment, and a completeness of coverage, which were all his own[72] — Gratian's purpose was to examine fearlessly the discrepancies between his grouped extracts, and then by means of distinction to reconcile them. His own title for this massive

69. The traditional date was 1151; but it has been accepted for some time that 1140 is nearer the mark — see, e.g. 1 RASHDALL 130, note 3, and the full title of *l'Age classique*, from which it would appear that the date 1150 at page 128 of that work (RAMBAUD) is a simple misprint.
70. KUTTNER, *Father* (1941) and *Graziano* (1953).
71. RAMBAUD (1965), pages 51 to 64.
72. *Op. cit.*, pages 64 to 69 (comment) and 78 to 99 (plan).

work, the "Concordance of Discordant Canons," reflects this better than its popular name, the *Decreta*.[73]

Each excerpt was called a "canon," or alternatively a "chapter" (*capitulum*), and is cited like a "law" of the civil corpus by its first words. But the excerpts were not collected into Titles and Books as in the civil Corpus: the first and shorter part of the Decreta groups them into "Distinctions," and the second and longer into "Causes," subdivided into "questions."[74] All these were identified by serial numbers, not by names. The length of the whole is about the same as Justinian's Code, rather under 400,000 words.

29. After Gratian. — The great work was hardly published before other hands took it over. Up till 1170[75] copyists were adding texts which Gratian (no doubt intentionally) had omitted, and these additions were early dubbed "*Paleæ*,"[76] no one can confidently say why. Extracts thought to be apposite from the civil Corpus found their way into the text,[77] and these were said to be "canonised" by their inclusion as "canons." His commentary also was enlarged in places by civilian additions, including an adaptation of a summula by Bulgarus[78] and a treatise on prescription attributed to James.[79] Finally two theological treatises, aberrantly named "Distinctions,"[80] were added: one is reckoned as an independent third part, and the other inserted among the "Causes" of the second part as a single (but subdivided) "question."

Apart from additions by copyists, the Decreta were glossed before 1148 by one POCAPAGLIA (Paucapalea),[81] of whom nothing is known except that he taught canon law at Bologna; and they received an Apparatus from a CARDINAL, who would appear[82] to be identical with HUBALD, cardinal from 1141 to at least 1149. Meanwhile, between

73. Not *Decretum* in the singular till comparatively recent times — KUTTNER, *Father*, at page 15. The singular in any case makes no sense.
74. For the third part, added later, see note 69 below.
75. RAMBAUD, page 118.
76. *Op. cit.*, pages 100 to 114.
77. For argument that Gratian himself was not responsible for these, see RAMBAUD, pages 119 to 126.
78. KANTOROWICZ, *Studies*, at page 80.
79. *Op. cit.*, at page 79.
80. *de Consecratione* and *de Penitentia*, RAMBAUD, pages 90 to 99 and 82 to 90.
81. R. NAZ, (1957), 6 Naz 1268.
82. Rudolf WEIGAND, *Die Glossen des Cardinals*, (1973) 3 Bulletin of Medieval Canon Law 73, at pages 92 to 95. It used to be thought that "the Cardinal" was another Gratian, who died in 1190, and the Apparatus was dated to 1160 or so.

1143 and 1145, ROLAND BANDINELLI[83] published a short commentary (about 50,000 words, nearly all on the second part) which he called "Jottings" (*Stromata*). Master Roland taught both canon law and theology at Bologna until he was made cardinal in 1150. In theology he had been a student of the same Abelard whose influence is noticeable on Gratian's method. The year after Roncaglia he was elected pope by the anti-imperial party as Alexander III (1159-1181). Two other early teachers, both of them up to 1157, were OGNIBENE (*Omnibonus*),[84] Bishop of Verona from that date till his death in 1185, and ALBERT di MORA of Benevento,[85] cardinal from that date and pope for some months as Gregory VIII in 1187. The era of the lawyer-popes had begun.

30. "Legists" and "Canonists." — It was Gratian's systematisation and explanation of his sources that elevated the study of canon law to an intellectual discipline on the same level as the civil law. As Irnerius had cut the navel-string which bound the civil law to philosophy and rhetoric, so Gratian separated the study of canon law from that of theology. In this he was aided by the publication soon afterwards[86] of Peter Lombard's Sentences: their two mutually exclusive books became the bases of instruction in canon law and theology respectively, each driving out its predecessors.

The "canonists" disagreed with the "legists" (as the adepts of the two disciplines were called from their extracts being denominated canons and laws) on the ultimate superiority of Justinian's law, and hence of the Roman Emperor, a disagreement which found more incisive expression in the next generation. But this did not obscure the new discovery that both systems were species of the same genus,[87] instead of each being a species of some other genus. The discovery was consolidated by the identity of the language in which both were taught. This continued indeed to be Latin; but it was not the same Latin as before. The new science was a deliberate and enthusiastic revolt against

83. M. PACAUT, (1965) 7 Naz 702.
84. R. CHABANNE, (1957) 6 Naz 1111.
85. KUTTNER, *Bernardus*, at page 282.
86. Between 1150 and 1152: 1 RASHDALL, page 259 (his editors).
87. The doctors of the two disciplines formed separate *collegia* (guilds, we might say faculties) certainly at a later date — 1 RASHDALL 147 — perhaps always. Rashdall has a reference from 1215 to the doctors of both collectively, but also one to a "universitas" of masters *and* scholars, which in the technical sense of an association seems never to have existed. As for the students, their *universitates* never differentiated between civil and canon law — 1 RASHDALL 149 and following.

the rhetorical approach characterising the liberal arts,[88] and the principal external sign of the revolt was the change of literary style. The most complicated ideas were expounded in a style so uncompromisingly simple as sometimes to give the impression even of childishness: no impression could be more deceptive.

88. It seems to have been Placentine (paragraph 36 below) who first said that "we have not to learn but to unlearn their teaching." Echoed by Azzo, this epigram gained universal currency — KANTOROWICZ, *Studies,* at page 58 — and what law teacher would disagree today?

Chapter III

Overall Views

(1150 - 1200)

The Summa

31. Meaning of Summa. — Meanwhile treatises had begun to appear on the whole of the law (civil or canon) rather than on single subjects in isolation. But the advance was more apparent than real, for the SUMMA (as such a treatise was called) was only a series of *Summule*, themselves commentaries on selected Titles in any one member of the Corpus, and arranged in the order of that member. No attempt was made, and within this self-imposed limitation none could be made, to group the Titles in wider categories; for the Books of the Institutes, still less of the Code, do not afford these. For more thoroughgoing systematisation, forsaking perforce Justinian's order, the civil law had to wait till the seventeenth century in France.

Canon law was in this respect in better case. It was saddled with no authoritative order; Gratian's was already better than Justinian's; and as we shall see presently (paragraph 45 below) nothing prevented a further re-arrangement.

32. Vienna Summa, Troyes Summa. — The first two civilian Summae are called (from the place where the leading manuscript is found) the Vienna Summa (*Vindobonensis*) and the Troyes Summa (*Trecensis*). Both were composed at Bologna, but neither indicates its author. The former, most untypically "prolix, slovenly and incoherent,"[1] was on the Institutes in 70,000 words; the latter, "concise but clumsy and monotonous,"[2] was hardly longer, dealing with about half the 550 Titles

---

1. The epithets are PATETTA's, at page 125 (427), as translated by KANTOROWICZ, *Studies*, at page 67. Cf. MEIJERS, *Sommes*, pages 216 to 219.
2. KANTOROWICZ, *Studies*, at page 172.

in the first nine Books of the Code. The opinions in the former are mostly those of Bulgarus, while those in the latter are wholly Martin's.[3] Of the former it can be said that it is earlier than the *Lectura* on the Institutes (paragraph 24 above) giving Martin's latest views, since the *Lectura* assumes knowledge of this Summa. The latter can be dated to about 1150.[4] It is therefore not clear which can claim the honour of being the earliest of its kind — if we do not count Roland's *Stromata* (1143-45, paragraph 29 above) on the Decreta.

33. Rufinus and Stephen. — Assuming that the "legists" were first with the Summa, it was not by much. A Summa on the Decreta was published between 1157 and 1159 by RUFINUS,[5] who may have studied under Gratian, and who certainly taught canon law at Bologna. His Summa (about 170,000 words) was more than three times the length of Roland's *Stromata*, and was of the kind distinguished as "exegetic," meaning that besides summarising the broad lines of the subject matter it also analysed the text like a later "Commentary." It was Rufinus who expressed most vividly the theory of papal superiority over the emperor by distinguishing their respective powers as *auctoritas* and *administratio* — authority and mere management. Like many, if not most, canonists he went early out of circulation as a teacher and writer, becoming bishop of Assisi perhaps even before the appearance of his Summa. He pronounced the opening allocution at the Third Council of the Lateran in 1179, and died as Archbishop of Sorrento some time before 1192.

In about 1160 another Summa was published, by STEPHEN, later bishop of TOURNAI (*Stephanus Tornacensis*),[6] who had studied at Bologna under Bulgarus and Rufinus. This Summa was again "exegetic," and much influenced by his master's, but only half his length. Stephen was French by origin, and would seem to have been about 25 years old when his Summa was published — at Orléans, because he had entered the chapter regular of St Euverte there five years earlier. He does not seem to have added teaching to his writing; but if he did he was soon removed from it by preferment: he became Abbot of St

3. MEIJERS, *Sommes,* page 219 and following, shows that in all but two of the cases where the Troyes Summa expresses views contrary to those attributed to Martin in the *Vetus Collectio Dissensionum Dominorum,* that attribution is wrong. In the remaining two cases the *Lectura* mentioned at paragraph 24 above omits them, which may mean that Martin had abandoned them before he died.
4. KANTOROWICZ, *Studies,* at pages 43 and 164.
5. R. BENSON, (1965) 7 Naz 779.
6. G LEPOINTE, (1953) 5 Naz 487.

Euverte in 1167, Abbot of Ste Geneviève at Paris in 1176, Bishop of Tournai in 1191, and died in 1203.

34. Roger. — To come back to the "legists," no one in this third generation is described as a student of anyone but Bulgarus; but this may perhaps be only an acknowledgment that Bulgarus was head of the school. Certain it is that Martin's attitude did not die with him, those who carried on his views being dubbed Gosians from his surname.[7] The earliest of these, expressly said to have been a student of Bulgarus, preferred to call himself ROGER,[8] though others called him Froger: this was probably his real name, and has an equally respectable nordic root. Roger's birth-place seems to have been Piacenza, but he studied at Bologna (perhaps contemporaneously with Hugh and James), and must also have taught there, for large numbers of his glosses were recorded. Shortly after 1162 he went to Provence, perhaps to Arles but more probably to MONTPELLIER: Montpellier had been famous for a generation for its school of medicine, but there was no question of an earlier law-school there. Roger died about 1170.

His writings include at least three compositions called *Questiones Legitime*,[9] differing from the *Questiones Disputate* (above, paragraph 15) not only in their "literary" style — far different from the dry precision of the lawyers — but also in their contents. They were in the form of dialogues between Roger himself (by name) and *Jurisprudentia*, meaning Jurisprudence in the sense which it has kept in modern English, of general legal learning: Roger attacks the law for its inconsistencies, and Jurisprudence patiently reconciles them. Of the three, two were apparently written in Provence.[10]

Tradition is emphatic[11] in attributing to Roger the first Summa on the Code. Since the first Summa was the Gosian Troyes Summa, did Roger write that? He certainly left unfinished at his death a Summa specifically entitled *Summa Frogerii*; but this is quite evidently an expanded and much improved development of the Troyes Summa.[12] If Roger was indeed the author of the Troyes Summa (1150, paragraph 32 above), he has a good claim to have been the inventor of the Summa form. The *Summa Frogerii*, like the Troyes Summa but unlike his

7. KANTOROWICZ, *Studies*, at page 88.
8. *Op. cit.*, at pages 122 to 127 and 180.
9. *Op. cit.*, at pages 127 to 142.
10. *Op. cit.*, at page 10.
11. *Op. cit.*, at page 166: Odofred (died in 1265) says so four times.
12. *Op. cit.*, at pages 166 to 171. MEIJERS disagreed, *l'Equité et la loi* (1941), at page 145, note 17.

Questiones, was in the direct "legal" style; and its abandonment of the more extreme Gosian views of the Troyes Summa is no argument against identity of authorship: Roger had grown up by twenty years. So far as it went, the new Summa was twice as long as the old; but Roger did not quite reach the half-way mark before he died.[13] Perhaps because it was unfinished, it was the earlier version that was translated somewhat freely into Provençal about 1170[14] as *Lo Codi,* and was very influential in southern France for a long time.

35. Exceptiones Petri. — Roger was not the only law teacher in southern France at this time: we have seen above that the Catalan churchman Peter of Cardona was there from the middle of the century till he received his cardinal's hat in 1166; and his translation of a Greek "constitution" in the Code was used by one PETER, teacher at the law-school at Valence, when he published an epitome of the whole of Roman law called Peter's Excerpts (*Exceptiones Petri*).[15] This Peter was influenced by the Bologna glossators, particularly by Martin's views on the Institutes, but he was very independent. His grouping of the whole of the law into four Books, dealing with Persons, Contract, Delict and Actions, was one example of his independence and had no imitators: Bologna was too engrossed in detail to raise her sights to this extent.

36. Placentine. — Though again formally a student of Bulgarus, PLACENTINE[16] was also under the influence of Roger. His personal name may perhaps have been Savinus, *Placentinus* meaning simply "of Piacenza." After his studies at Bologna he went to Mantua and taught there from about 1160: he was an Italian patriot with both contempt for and resentment against the rude but strong Germans, and his departure may have had some connection with Roncaglia.[17] It is a plausible theory, but not unchallenged, that he was the author at this

13. The *Summa Tubingensis* is the *Summa Frogerii* completed from the Troyes Summa. Manuscript Vich 156 (formerly 82) carried the *Summa Frogerii* completed by Placentine (paragraph 36 below) — KANTOROWICZ, *Studies,* at page 148. Cf. MEIJERS, *Sommes,* at pages 219 to 231. For the length and quality see KANTOROWICZ, *Studies,* pages 172 and 173.
14. KANTOROWICZ, *Studies,* page 173; but for a possible earlier date see R. FEENSTRA in (1967) 13 Studia Gratiana, pages 65 to 67.
15. KANTOROWICZ, *Exceptiones Petri* (1937), and *Studies,* pages 112 to 118, must now be read subject to WEIMAR, *Entstehung* (1972). Kantorowicz dated this work to soon after 1110, and even earlier dates have been vigorously defended.
16. KANTOROWICZ, *Poetical Sermon* (1938-39), to page 26 (115). See also Ch. LEFEBVRE, (1965) 7 Naz 1.
17. He denounced with passionate vituperation the advice which the Four Doctors gave there — KANTOROWICZ, *Studies,* at page 194.

point of the passionately anti-German *Questiones de Juris Subtilitatibus*[18] "questions" in Roger's style, and making use of one of those which Roger wrote in Provence but naming the parties *Interpres* and *Auditor.* Placentine was the undoubted author, in the early 1160s, of a famous treatise on the different kinds of action, the *Libellus de Varietate Actionum* which has an affinity with these "Questions."

It seems likely that he went back to Bologna before leaving in about 1170 for Montpellier, having probably enough been invited to succeed Roger there. There he first wrote an end to Roger's unfinished Summa on the Code, and then a new beginning to replace Roger's. His complete Summa thus constituted is more than three times the length of the Troyes Summa, something under 250,000 words. He also wrote a Summa on the Institutes. Placentine was of an independent and eclectic turn of mind, agreeing with Bulgarus as often as with Martin — he wrote annotations (*additiones*) to Bulgarus' apparatus on the last title of the Digest (*de Regulis Juris*) — but it was as a Gosian that he was remembered, particularly by the later canonists who were indebted to him for part of their theory of "equity."

He returned to Piacenza in about 1185, perhaps because of the Peace of Constance, and taught there and at Bologna till 1191. Then he went back to Montpellier and died there a year later, leaving unfinished a Summa on the last "Three Books" of the Code.

37. Canonists at Bologna. — Among the canonists contemporary with Placentine, mention must be made of GANDULF,[19] who appears to have been teaching at Bologna from 1160 to 1185 or so: no work of his has survived, but his opinions were much cited.

In 1171 appeared the third Bolognese Summa on the Decreta, by JOHN OF FAENZA (*Joannes Faventinus*):[20] it was not original, merely reproducing Rufinus and Stephen, but in reproducing them it displaced them. John taught canon law at Bologna, and was the author of many glosses in which he refers back to his Summa. Like Placentine among the "legists," John was the odd man out among the canonists, being a partisan of the Emperor: the increasing unpopularity of this cause was perhaps the reason for his withdrawal about 1174 to his native Faenza, where he died a canon about 1187.[21]

---

18. KANTOROWICZ, *Studies,* pages 181 to 205.
19. Ch. LEFEBVRE, (1953) 5 Naz 933.
20. A.M. STICKLER, (1957) 6 Naz 99.
21. He is not the same as Bishop John of Faenza, who died in 1191. — KUTTNER, *Bernardus* (1943), at page 281, note 11.

Finally in this series is the Summa on the Decreta by SIMON of BISIGNANO,[22] soon after 1174. Simon had learnt his canon law at Bologna, apparently from Gratian, and probably taught there. The novelty of his Summa lies in the extensive use made of papal decretals issued since Gratian.

38. Northern France and England. — From about 1160 canon-law works had been appearing in a more rhetorical style in many places in northern France, and as far afield as the Rhineland.[23] They included Summae, collections of Distinctions and (a little later) of Problems (*Questiones*), and treatises on procedure: these were all anonymous. It was in northern France, it will be remembered, that Stephen's Summa appeared about 1160, but it was purely Bolognese in inspiration and style. This was not the case with its contemporary, the "exegetic" and much longer "Paris" Summa[24] (*Magister Gratianus...*, over 150,000 words), which does not appear to have been influenced by Stephen's. Its author had added to the study of the law at Bologna that of theology and rhetoric at Paris.

This combination of studies was not uncommon, and was shared by the Carinthian author of the "Munich" Summa (*Imperatorie Majestati...*) published between 1175 and 1178. This was a "simple" Summa, meaning that it dealt with principles only, instead of expounding the words of the text as well: it deserves mention because it influenced Huguccio (paragraph 42 below).

But this does not mean that the law was not taught at Paris: the author of the "Paris" Summa himself taught there. The teaching of civil law was also firmly established by 1170 or so:[25] there would appear to be no earlier evidence, and in any case no civilian teaching or writing at Paris at this time would contribute to the general current of development. It is at least clear that (quite the opposite of the position at Bologna) both faculties were numerically insignificant beside the enormous but "inferior" faculty of arts, as was the other "superior" faculty, that of theology. The teaching of arts and theology had continued without a break since the days of Abelard; but there is no sign before this same date of 1170[26] of the organisation of the youthful Masters of Arts, like

---

22. R.P.A. LAMBERT, (1937) 2 Naz 900.
23. KUTTNER, *Débuts* (1938).
24. Edited by MCLAUGHLIN (Toronto, 1952), who dates it soon after 1160 because it is not influenced by Stephen.
25. Evidence for 1173, supported by another reference between 1170 and 1190, in KANTOROWICZ, *Studies*, at page 10.
26. 1 RASHDALL, 292.

the mature students of law at Bologna, into what would become the University.

With PETER of BLOIS (*Petrus Blesensis*)[27] the Younger we come to names: influenced both by Gandulf and by the "Munich" Summa, he wrote Distinctions at Chartres about 1180, and also an *Ordo Judiciarius*. At the same time SICARD of CREMONA[28] wrote at Mainz a "simple" Summa, the result of his teaching in France since 1170. He had studied at Bologna, and laid under contribution both the "Munich" Summa and Simon of Bisignano. Sicard went back to Italy, became bishop of his native town in 1185, and died in 1215.

Clerks based in England, then culturally part of northern France, were playing some part in this development. An early "simple" Summa, following Stephen, was the work of ODO of DOVER (*Dourensis*);[29] and the turbulent GERALD de BARRI (*Giraldus Cambrensis*) taught at Paris between 1176 and 1180. Between 1183 and 1189 WILLIAM de LONGCHAMPS (later Richard I's Chancellor and bishop of Ely, who died in 1197) published what appears to be the first comparative treatise, on civil-law and canon-law procedure together: the *Practica Legum et Decretorum*.

39. John Bassian. — To return to Bologna, the third Summa on the Code was written by JOHN BASSIAN (*Joannes Bassianus*)[30] about 1180,[31] still before the Peace of Constance. John was a student of Bulgarus, and (unlike those previously mentioned) faithfully carried on his master's views. He did not die till towards the end of the century; and the principal object of his long teaching life, unhampered as were the canonists by ecclesiastical preferment, was to beat down Gosianism and to re-establish strict fidelity to the Roman texts. In this he was to all appearance very successful;[32] but the intellectually venturesome are slippery opponents, and as we shall see later their views were merely driven underground.

John's Summa on the Code, written to drive out Placentine's,[33] was not in fact complete, nor was the Summa which he composed for

27. R.P.A. LAMBERT, (1937) 2 Naz 925, supplemented by Ch. LEFEBVRE, (1957) 6 Naz 1472.
28. Ch. LEFEBVRE, (1965) 7 Naz 1007.
29. KUTTNER, *Anglo-Norman Canonists* (1949-1951), at page 293, note 11.
30. He has been confused, and by those who should have known better, with the glossator BAZIANUS, of whom nothing is known except that he worked at Bologna and died a canon there in 1197 — KUTTNER, *Bernardus*, at pages 293, 294.
31. KANTOROWICZ, *Studies*, at page 44.
32. MEIJERS, *Sommes*, at page 244.
33. MEIJERS, *Sommes*, at page 233.

the same purpose on the Institutes. His Summa on the Authenticum seems to have been;[34] but on the Digest (a new departure) his work amounted to no more than summulae.[35] More complete were the notes of his lectures on the Institutes, Code and Digest recorded by his student NICOLAS the MADMAN (*Furiosus*),[36] following the example of William di Cabriano on Bulgarus. John is the first of the glossators recorded as having given a "consultation,"[37] an OPINION like the *responsa* of Roman times on an actual dispute before a court.

40. Minor Contemporaries. — AUBREY of the RAVENNA GATE (*Albericus de Porta Ravennate*) in Bologna was another of Bulgarus' students, famous in his time for his "Distinctions."[38] Other contemporaries of John Bassian, who are hardly more than names, were CYPRIAN[39] and OTTO of PAVIA (*Papiensis*):[40] the latter is said to have studied under Placentine and to have written an *Ordo Judiciarius*.

An anonymous student of Placentine was the author of another discussion of contradictions between "laws," the so-called VENDOME SUMMA (*Summa Vindocinensis* or *Summa Contrarietatum*).[41]

41. Pillio. — But Placentine's best-known student was another stormy petrel, PILLIO (*Pillius* or *Pileus*) of MEDICINA, a township under Bologna.[42] He was in practice at the bar as early as 1169 and last mentioned in 1207. Those who taught at Bologna were made to take an oath not to teach elsewhere; but at some time before 1182 Pillio marked his discontent by a "secession" (in which he was followed by his students) to MODENA, less than 25 miles away but in Lombardy. Besides the usual glossing he composed a series of PROBLEMS

34. MEIJERS, *Droit féodal* (1934), at page 263.
35. MEIJERS, *Sommes*, at page 233.
36. These *lecturæ* on the Institutes and Code (first nine Books) have been discovered; but on the Digest only fragments on the Old and the New — MEIJERS, *Sommes*, at pages 237 to 239 and 245 to 257.
37. MEIJERS, *Droit féodal*, at page 262.
38. 4 SAVIGNY 225 and following.
39. *Op. cit.*, at page 354.
40. *Op. cit.*, at pages 377 and following.
41. Described by MEIJERS, *Sommes*, at page 236. E. SECKEL's study on this work, *Die Summa Vindocinensis*, is edited by E. GENZMER in Abhandlungen der Preussische Akademie Wissenschafts, 1939, phil.-hist. K1. III (Berlin, 1939).
42. Ch. LEFEBVRE, (1937) 6 Naz 1499. The authority for the location of Medicina is Odofred (paragraph 65 below), cited at 1 SARTI 83. For his Questiones see Ugo NICOLINI, *Pilii Medicinensis Quæstiones Sabbatinæ: Introduzione all' Edizione Critica* (1933); and KANTOROWICZ, *Quæstiones* (1939), pages 14, 15 and passim.

(*Questiones*, or *Brocarda* as he called them) in the same form as the earlier recording of moot court proceedings — statement of the problem in the interrogative, arguments for and against (*pro, contra*, hence perhaps *bro-carda*) and judgment — but they were written by the master himself with no intention of faithfully recording a debate which had actually taken place, though discussion in class, or a case argued in court, might be the origin of the problem. It would seem that this work was composed before 1187; and of the two rescensions of another work entitled *Libellus Disputatorius* one may be earlier than this, while the second is to be dated to 1195: this book dealt with questions of evidence and procedure and included a collection of "distinctions." After Placentine's death in 1192, Pillio continued, but did not finish, his Summa on the Three Books.

Pillio was the earliest legist to go outside Roman law (after his departure from Bologna) to comment on the feudal customary law.[43] These customs had been reduced to writing in the middle of the century by two letters of OBERTO dall' ORTO, judge of the imperial court at Milan, to his son when a student at Bologna, and later supplemented; but the Bolognese doctors had so far ignored them.[44] Pillio first wrote a Summa on this collection, and then started an Apparatus, which he did not finish: both were apparently earlier than the *Liber Disputatorius* (above).

Pillio also adventured in canon law: citations from the Decreta are not uncommon. And he was twice of counsel in the papal court for the monks of Canterbury: in 1187 against their Archbishop;[45] and in 1205 against King John in the disputed election to the Archbishopric.[46]

42. Huguccio. — The definitive monument of the Bolognese decretists was the "exegetic" Summa of HUGUCCIO of PISA,[47] left not quite finished in 1188. Huguccio was himself influenced by the "Munich" Summa (paragraph 38 above); but, as is more often the case with the early canonists than with the "legists," it is not certain who his master had been. It is possible that Albert di Mora (Pope Gregory VIII above)

---

43. MEIJERS, *Droit féodal*, at pages 263 to 269.
44. This did not prevent their voicing opinions on feudal controversies: MEIJERS, at pages 261 to 263 of the same article.
45. 1 POLLOCK and MAITLAND, *History of English Law* 121 (reissue of 1968).
46. KUTTNER, *Bernardus*, at pages 326, note 30.
47. A.M. STICKLER, (1965) 7 Naz 1355. Cf. LEONARDI, *Vita e opera di Uguccione da Pisa*, (1956-1957) 4 Studia Gratiana 45. "Huguccio" is spelt in many different ways: it is diminutive of Hugh, and he himself signed when Bishop as *Ego Ugo Ferrariensis Episcopus* — LEONARDI, *loc. cit.*, at page 50.

was one of them; and it is certain that Huguccio both studied and taught at Bologna. Among his students was that dynamic nobleman Lothario di Segni, the future Pope Innocent III (1198-1216). Huguccio became Bishop of Ferrara in 1190, and so remained till his death in 1210.

43. England — In the last twenty years of the century clerks from England were not merely involved in the north French current. Canon law was being taught in England, probably at Oxford alongside Vacarius' civilian school: some names are known, but the independent tradition did not continue.[48]

It was at Paris that RICHARD ENGLISH (*Ricardus Anglicus*)[49] was teaching canon law in 1186 and 1187, publishing at this stage a *Summa Questionum.* This meant a collection of the problems which he had put to his students for their discussion in class and his solution: the "problem-method" is not such a novelty as some people think. He was then briefly in England, where it is suggested that he may have made contact with Vacarius or his successors before going still further away to Bologna. At Bologna he stayed for most of the last decade of the century, teaching and writing; but in 1202 he became Prior of Dunstable, and remained in that office till his death in 1242. Among the intellectual baggage which he took with him to Bologna was no doubt the north-French predilection for procedure: he published the first[50] Bolognese treatise on canon-law procedure (*Ordo Judiciarius*) in 1196. He also published two works on the Decreta (*Distinctiones* and *Argumenta* or *Notabilia*), followed by *Casus* and an Apparatus on the Decretals, for the recently established course on which he seems to have been responsible.

44. Decretals. — For canon lawyers had now other hares to hunt than the Decreta. Papal pronouncements had continued to issue since 1140: they might have been called Novels by analogy with the civil law, but the name they were in fact given was *Decretales Extravagantes* as "wandering outside" the Decreta. They had been largely ignored by the north-French school;[51] but they engaged the attention of the Bologna canonists, several of whom made collections of them.

---

48. KUTTNER, *Anglo-Norman Canonists,* at pages 317 to 327.
49. KUTTNER, *Anglo-Norman Canonists* (1949-1951), at pages 327 to 339, and *Ricardus Anglicus,* (1965) 7 Naz 676. Richard's surname outside canon-law teaching was de Mores; and "English" was not a surname but a nickname. It is given in this form (instead of "the English" or "the Englishman") by analogy with the well-accepted form "Peter Lombard," and also because this sort of nickname became this sort of surname not so long after.
50. A.M. STICKLER, *Ordines Judiciarii,* (1957) 6 Naz 1132, at Column 1137.
51. KUTTNER, *Débuts* (1938), at page 203.

45. Bernard of Pavia. — All these collections were superseded by the *Breviarium Extravagantium* composed by BERNARD of PAVIA (*Papiensis*)[52] between 1188 and 1192: he was then Provost (*prepositus,* nearly the same as Dean) of the cathedral of his native town. Bernard had studied under John of Faenza,[53] and had been teaching at Bologna[54] and glossing the Decreta for the last fifteen years. Besides the Decretals newly issued in the past half-century he included much matter from earlier days which Gratian had omitted; and he set the future fashion by arranging his extracts according to subject matter in five Books, each divided into Titles like the civil law. The individual extracts, cited by their first words, were neither "laws" nor "canons," but "chapters," *capitula.* While Bishop of Faenza (1191 to 1198) Bernard went on to compose a short Summa (less than 60,000 words). It is properly called *Summa Decretalium* because it follows the order of his Breviary; but it deals with the whole of canon law and not merely the Decretals. The Summa has no great originality: its virtue lies in its clarity. After translation to Pavia, which see he occupied till his death in 1213, Bernard composed *Casus* on the Decretals, making use of Richard's work of the same name. He was one of the very few ecclesiastics to continue to write after preferment.

---

52. G. LE BRAS, (1937) 2 Naz 782; KUTTNER, *Bernardus* (1943), at pages 295 to 299.
53. Not Huguccio — KUTTNER, *Bernardus,* at page 295, note 23.
54. Before 1179 he had written two Summulae (*de Matrimonio* and *de Electione*), and had made an earlier collection of Decretals, now called the *Collectio Parisiensis IIa* — KUTTNER, *Bernardus,* at pages 295 and 296.

Chapter IV

The Zenith

(1200 - 1265)

Definitive Summa and Standard Gloss

46. Hugolin. — John Bassian had many students faithful to his orthodox line.[1] We have already referred to Nicolas the Madman who recorded John's own lectures; and JAMES DOVE (*Jacobus Columbi*)[2] completed Placentine's Summa on the Three Books, left unfinished by Pillio, as well as Pillio's own unfinished Apparatus on the *Liber Feudorum*.

A greater man was HUGOLIN,[3] who, besides glosses amounting to regular Apparatus on all members of the Corpus except the Authenticum, wrote a Summa on the Digest incorporating the fragments that John had left.[4] He made a collection of 52 Problems (*questiones insolubiles*), but probably not of the 470-odd *Dissensiones Dominorum* that have been attributed to him. He was still alive in 1233.

47. Azzo. — Greatest of all was AZZO[5] (*Azo* in Latin: it is a nordic root, perhaps corresponding to the English "Ed" for Edward, not the Latin *Actius*). First mentioned as *doctor legum* in 1190, he set out to complete John's fragmentary Summa on the Code, but abandoned this

1. MEIJERS, *Sommes,* at page 233.
2. MEIJERS, *Sommes,* at page 241, and *Droit féodal* (1934), at pages 269 and 270. *Columbi* is a patronymic, son of Columbus: his father's name and nickname were Geoffrey Dove (*Goffredus Columbus*). Cf. 5 SAVIGNY 89 to 98.
3. 5 SAVIGNY 45 to 68; KANTOROWICZ, *Quæstiones* (1939), pages 16, 17 (148, 149), *Greek Justinian* (1945), page 49 (190).
4. MEIJERS, *Sommes,* at page 233, note 84; KANTOROWICZ, *Studies,* at page 39. note 12.
5. P. FIORELLI, (1962) 4 D.B.I. 774; and 5 SAVIGNY, 1 to 34.

venture to publish his own[6] between 1208 and 1210.[7] This fourth Summa, at over half a million words, was twice the length of Placentine's; but a fair amount of the increase is due to the multiplication of references which had now become — and was to remain — the fashion. This Summa was the last of the series, and was never superseded throughout the Middle Ages. As late as the sixteenth century twenty-four different printed editions have been counted:[8] the printed editions usually supplement it with the Summa on the Three Books begun by Placentine.

Azzo also wrote a Summa on the Institutes; and of the wealth of glosses due to him those on the Old Digest[9] and on the Code amount to regular Apparatus. His lectures on the Code, recorded by an otherwise unknown student, have also by pure accident survived.[10] He died in 1220.[11]

48. Charles di Tocco. — Both John and Placentine, not to mention Cyprian and Otto of Pavia, were masters of CHARLES di TOCCO (*Karolus de Tocco*) of Benevento.[12] His glosses on the first four Books of the Code were added to those of his predecessors from Irnerius down to form a composite Apparatus.[13] After leaving his chair at Bologna for the bench at Salerno he glossed the *Lombarda*: Lombard law was still at home in southern Italy, uncontaminated by the Frankish influence which Charlemagne's conquest had inflicted on it in the north. This work was not finished till after 1215.

49. Bernard of Compostella the Elder. — In 1208 the so-called *Collectio Romana* of Pope Innocent III's decretals from 1198 to date was compiled by BERNARD of COMPOSTELLA the Elder.[14] Very little is known of this Spaniard, except that his master in civil law had been Azzo; that he glossed the other Bernard's "Breviary" in 1205 and 1206, and then and later was glossing the Decreta; and that he taught canon

6. MEIJERS, *Sommes,* at page 234 and note 85.
7. KANTOROWICZ, *Studies,* at page 44.
8. MEIJERS, *Sommes,* at page 234.
9. KANTOROWICZ, *Studies,* at page 52.
10. MEIJERS, *Sommes,* at page 240.
11. So the chronicler Albéric de Trois Fontaines. Savigny thought this impossible, for reasons which are criticised by Fiorelli (note 5 above), and suggested 1230.
12. 5 SAVIGNY, 174 to 183.
13. P. LEGENDRE, (1957) 34 R.H.D.F.E., 413, at note 3. Savigny thought it was a Commentary by Charles' student Roffred — 5 SAVIGNY, at page 196 — because he misread the *siglum* .K. as .R. MEIJERS, *Sommes,* at page 240, corrected the attribution, but still regarded it as a Commentary. If it were it would be the first of its kind.
14. KUTTNER, *Bernardus,* at pages 303 to 315.

law in the shortlived school of **Vicenza**. This school, which endured from 1204 to 1209,[15] was the first of a series of "secessions" from Bologna at this time. The *Collectio Romana* was disapproved by Innocent, who superseded it by the despatch of an official selection of his own Decretals (down to 1210) to "the whole of the masters and students sojourning at Bologna"[16] both for study and for application in court.

50. Other Bolognese Canonists. — The gap between the "Breviary" and Innocent's selection (1181 to 1198) was filled in the next year or two by a second Englishman teaching at Bologna, JOHN WALSH (*Joannes Galensis*):[17] no more is known of him. The three collections came to be known as the FIRST, SECOND and THIRD ANCIENT COMPILATIONS, that of John Walsh counting as the second by reason of the date of its contents, although it had been the third to appear.

The next few years showed a revival of Bolognese interest in the Decreta, with the appearance of four complete Apparatus,[18] all of them citing the Decretals where apposite. The first three of these four were those of ALAN, another Englishman of whom nothing is known (about 1210); of LAWRENCE SPANIARD (*Laurentius Hispanus*)[19] between 1210 and 1215, and an anonymous work known as the GLOSSA PALATINA, also between 1210 and 1215, frequently citing both Bernard of Compostella and Lawrence's earlier glosses. Lawrence too had studied civil law under Azzo: his canon-law master is as usual unknown. He went out of circulation in 1218 on his election to the bishopric of Orense, remaining there till his death in 1248.

51. John Dutch. — The last of the four Apparatus on the Decreta was composed by JOHN DUTCH (*Joannes Teutonicus*)[20] soon after 1215: it superseded the others and became the STANDARD GLOSS (*Glossa Ordinaria*), which meant[21] that "it could possibly be contradict-

---

15. 2 RASHDALL, pages 6 and 7.
16. *Universis magistris et scolaribus Bononie commorantibus* A. FRIEDBERG, *Quinque Compilationes Antiquæ* (1882, photographically reprinted in 1956), at page 105.
17. G. OESTERLE, (1957) 6 Naz 105. For the name see note 49 to Chapter III above on "Richard English." *Galensis* means "the Welsh," which gives the modern English surname Walsh.
18. KUTTNER, *Bernardus*, at pages 289 to 301.
19. A.M. STICKLER, (1957) 6 Naz 361.
20. S. STELLING-MICHAUD, (1957) 6 Naz 120; and compare KUTTNER, *Bernardus* (1943), at pages 291 and 292. John's country was probably Saxony, at any rate not the Low Countries; but "Dutch" is the philological equivalent of *Teutonicus, Deutsch*. In French he is called "Jean l'Allemand." His surname outside Bologna was Zemeke.
21. KUTTNER, *Bernardus*, at page 292.

ed, but had always to be considered first in the classroom interpretation of the Decreta as well as in the courts." This Apparatus was "received" north of the Alps, and no more is heard of a distinctively French school.[22] It also consigned to oblivion all former glossators on the Decreta, except Lawrence who is frequently cited. John Dutch again had studied civil law under Azzo: his canon-law master is unknown. He was perhaps the compiler of the FOURTH COMPILATION of Decretals, covering Innocent III's last six years; and he certainly provided both it and the Third Compilation with an Apparatus. He left Bologna in 1220 to spend the rest of his life (to 1245 or 1246) at Halberstadt in north Germany, as Provost first of the collegial chapter and from 1235 of the cathedral chapter: he died its Dean.

52. Tancred. — The Standard Gloss to the first three Compilations was provided by TANCRED,[23] another student under Azzo in the civil law: his canon-law masters were Lawrence Spaniard and John Walsh. Tancred is better known for his Treatise on Procedure (*Ordo Judiciarius*), in which he says he is following Richard English and Pillio.[24] This treatise was written between 1214, when he became *Magister Decretorum,* and 1216; and it held the field till 1271, when the *Speculum Judiciale* appeared (paragraph 77 below). Tancred became canon and Archdeacon of Bologna in 1226, and died in 1236.

53. Liber Extra. — In 1226 Pope Honorius sent the FIFTH COMPILATION, his own decretals over the preceding twelve years, to Tancred in his new capacity of Archdeacon of Bologna,[25] for use as before in classroom and court. An Apparatus was soon provided by JAMES of ALBENGA (*Albanensis*),[26] whose master is unknown: he appears as advocate in 1210, and was teaching at Bologna between 1220 and 1230. He seems to have expected to be elected Bishop of his native city, but to have failed.[27]

In 1234 Pope Gregory IX officially communicated to the masters and students of Bologna[28] a consolidation of all five compilations, in-

---

22. KUTTNER, *Débuts,* at pages 201, 203.
23. L. CHEVAILLER, (1965) 7 Naz 1146; and compare KUTTNER, *Bernardus,* at pages 277 and 308.
24. Though modern research is inclined to attribute to Bencivenne the *Ordo* fathered on Pillio — Ch. LEFEBVRE, *Pillius,* (1957) 6 Naz 1499.
25. FRIEDBERG, *Compilationes Antiquæ* (note 16 above), at page 151.
26. J. LIPS and H. WAGNON, (1957) 6 Naz 77.
27. That he was Bishop of Faenza appears to be a mistake — KUTTNER, *Bernardus,* at page 335, notes 21 and 22.
28. A. FRIEDBERG, *Corpus Juris Canonici* (1879, photographically reprinted 1959), Vol. II, cols. 1 and 2.

corporating most of their contents and superseding them, and adding some of his own. This is the LIBER EXTRAVAGANTIUM DECRETALIUM, always cited in the Middle Ages as "Extra." It preserved the arrangement invented by Bernard of Pavia in five Books, and is a good deal less in bulk than Gratian's Decreta which it supplemented, but still well over 300,000 words.

54. James Baldwin. — Among the elder of Azzo's students was JAMES BALDWIN (*Jacobus Balduini*),[29] who was by way of being a cuckoo in the nest. He was "jurisconsult" from 1210, doctor by 1213, and in his teaching openly differed from his master, even saying that one of his interpretations was "false." This stung the old man to retort that his ex-student was a "liar."[30] James had in fact been bitten by the Gosian heresy which John Bassian had thought to suppress: if he had left any considerable writing we might see that Azzo was not his only master; but scattered glosses and some small notes on procedure are all we possess. It is at least clear that it was not only in his opinions that he was a deviationist, but also in his dialectical and abstract approach.[31] He served for a year as Podestà (Mayor) of Genoa from 1229 to 1230, and carried through a general revision of the city's laws. He died in 1235, having passed on the flame (if orally) to several notable followers.

55. Outside Bologna. — This was the generation which saw the crumbling of Bologna's monopoly, though not yet of her primacy, in the civil law. Teachers of repute were active elsewhere, even in Italy. ALBERT of PAVIA (*Papiensis*)[32] taught continuously at Modena, perhaps in some sense as Pillio's successor, from at least 1211 to at least 1240. Among his students (and among his successors at Modena) was HOMOBONUS (Goodfellow) of CREMONA.[33] Apparently less continuous was the teaching at Parma of HUBERT of BOBBIO (*Bobiensis*),[34] whose master is equally unknown. Hubert taught at Parma from at least 1214 to 1228, and was teaching there again in 1237: he was dead by 1245.

---

29. LIOTTA, *Jacobus Balduini* (1964). "Balduini" means "son of Baldwin:" as a modern English surname this patronymic becomes "Baldwin."
30. The source of this story is naturally Odofred (paragraph 65 below).
31. MEIJERS, *Orléans* (1918, 1921), at 3 *Etudes*, page 114.
32. 1 SARTI 131; 5 SAVIGNY 78 and 79.
33. Who was in turn one of the masters of Hostiensis (paragraph 64 below) — 5 SAVIGNY 384-386.
34. 5 SAVIGNY 143-147. In view of the article on him by R. CHABANNE, (1965) 7 Naz 1355, it is necessary to emphasise that he was *not* a canonist, though like most legists he counted many churchmen among his students, and that he did not *become* Doctor of Laws at Parma in 1214.

In the interval he appears at Vercelli in Piedmont in 1228 (when he was consulted on behalf of St Louis' mother and regent) and at Modena in 1234. Apart from glosses he published in 1236[35] a *Libellus* containing advice to advocates on procedure; and he also made a collection of *Questiones*. Among his students were three who were to make their mark in France: at Parma Simon[36] who in 1260 became Chancellor of that kingdom and from 1281 to 1285 was Pope as Martin IV; at Modena, JOHN WHITE (*Joannes Blancus*, Jean Leblanc),[37] who on his return to practice at Marseilles wrote a remarkable *Summa de Feudis* (before 1262), and also a Treatise on Testamentary Executors. The third was a Lombard, Guy of Como, whom we shall meet later at the dawn of the law-school at Orleans[38] (paragraph 86 below).

The serenity of Bologna was also troubled by a series of "secessions," at first short-lived, like those to Vicenza from 1204 to 1209, and to Arezzo in Tuscany in 1215; but in 1222 there was a massive "secession" to PADUA[39] near Venice, where both civil and canon law had been taught for some time.[40] This must have involved close on half the student body, since in 1228 between 2,500 and 3,000 were ready to go on from Padua to Vercelli, perhaps attracted there by Hubert of Bobbio: a sober estimate of the numbers at Bologna at the turn of the century would be 8,000.[41] It is certain that some in fact went to Vercelli, and some stayed at Padua,[42] but little more is known of either group.

56. Naples and Rome. — Outside Italy the teaching of Roman law had been suppressed at Paris in 1219 and in England in 1234. There was more than one reason for both steps, but one seems to have been royal dislike for the Romanists' inflation of the Emperor.

The opposite reason had no doubt something to do with the founding of a *Studium Generale* by the Emperor Frederick II in 1224 at

35. 6 BETHMANN-HOLLWEG, *der Civilprozess des gemeinen Rechts*, i.155 (1874).
36. MEIJERS, *Orléans*, 3 *Etudes* at page 17.
37. MEIJERS, *Toulouse* (1938), 3 *Etudes* at page 169.
38. MEIJERS, *Orléans*, 3 *Etudes* at page 33.
39. 2 RASHDALL 10.
40. St Dominic, visiting Bologna in 1219, received two "brothers," one of Vercelli and the other of Piacenza, who "had" taught at Padua civil and canon law respectively: SORBELLI, *Padova prima del 1222* (1922), at page 119.
41. According to Odofred (paragraph 65 below) there were a good ten thousand law-students at Bologna at the turn of the century — 1 RASHDALL 180. For argument that this is a scribe's mistake for one thousand see P. FIORELLI, *Azzo*, (1962) 4 D.B.I. 774 — but this is hardly acceptable in view of the numbers ready to go from Padua to Vercelli (above, in the text).
42. 2 RASHDALL 12 and 13.

NAPLES: Frederick had inherited the Norman kingdom through his mother in 1197, and had been elected to his father's empire in 1214. The Pope not submitting to this encirclement, strife between the two powers was fierce and continuous until Frederick's death in 1250 dissolved the union between north and south. Meanwile in 1244 or 1245[43] Pope Innocent IV (paragraph 62 below) imitated his adversary by founding a *Studium Generale* attached to the ROMAN COURT (*Curia Romana*) and teaching principally the two laws.

The first years of the foundation at Naples are not too clear; but it is thought that civil law was taught from the beginning by a Beneventan BENEDICT of ISERNIA,[44] who had studied at Bologna under Hugolin and had been doctor since 1221. He continued to teach at Naples till at least 1252, and his glosses were cited at Bologna.

57. Roffred. — It is possible that ROFFRED, another Beneventan who had studied at Bologna, this time under Azzo and his fellow-countryman Charles di Tocco,[45] was also teaching at Naples from the beginning;[46] but this is far from certain.[47] He had been responsible for the secession in 1215 to Arezzo, where one of his students had been the eminent Neapolitan Pier della Vigna,[48] but he seems to have spent the rest of his life (from 1217) at Benevento: his appearance in other places was due to his widespread practice at the bar. Though never formally either in imperial or in papal service, he frequently rendered professional service to both sides, and at different periods he was more closely connected with one than with the other: it seems to have made a difference which side was master of Benevento. In 1235[49] he published an *Ordo Judiciarius* composed of *Libelli Juris Civilis* (pleadings in civil law), which were probably not so much fictitious specimens as selections from his own pleadings.[50] Immediately afterwards he published his 44 *Questiones Sabbatine* (Saturday Problems), culled from his

43. 2 RASHDALL 28. This *Studium* is to be distinguished from the later foundation of the *City* of Rome, and also, during the Avignon captivity of the papacy, from that of the City of Avignon.
44. *Iuris Interpretes Sæculi XIII* (Naples, 1924), pages 1 to 5. Mistranscription of this learned gentleman's name has given rise to much confusion: the most extreme is a mythical Peter of Ireland (*P. de Hybernia*).
45. MEIJERS, *Sommes,* at page 240. Owing to Savigny's mistaken attribution to Roffred of Charles di Tocco's Apparatus (note 13 above) Roffred is usually credited with study under all Charles' masters too.
46. MEIJERS, *Naples,* (1924) at page 154.
47. Giovanni FERRETTI, *Roffredo Epifanio da Benevento,* (1908-1911) 3 Studi Medievali 255.
48. *Loc. cit.,* at page 266 and 267, note 8.
49. *Loc. cit.,* at page 272.
50. *Loc. cit.,* at page 234.

two years at Arezzo and inspired by Pillio's *Questiones*.[51] He began a compilation of canon-law pleadings on which he was still working when overtaken by death,[52] some time after 1243.[53]

58. Martin of Fano. — Another of Azzo's students, and another who taught outside Bologna, was MARTIN of FANO,[54] of whose life nothing is known between 1229 and 1255: at the earlier date he was teaching in his home-town of Fano, and at the latter he exchanged Arezzo for Modena. In 1260 he was (like James Baldwin before him) Podestà of Genoa, and again in 1262. He left many treatises, nearly all on procedure, which were still cited several generations later.

59. Accursius. — Contempt was the attitude of the Florentine ACCURSIUS[55] towards these schools outside Bologna. He had himself studied under Azzo at Bologna, and remained there to teach from about 1215 alongside James Baldwin.

In the century and a quarter since Irnerius had founded the law-school at Bologna so many glosses had been written that no one without an almost superhuman degree of perseverance could find his way through the wood. Accursius had this perseverance. He selected, transcribed, condensed and conflated all that he thought worth while in his predecessors' work on the whole of the Corpus Juris, and for good measure threw in many comments of his own. The Apparatus of Azzo and of Hugolin were his predominant sources,[56] but he neglected none. The Gosians were not excluded in favour of *nostri doctores,* as the more orthodox were called, though their views were often cited to be rejected. The individual glosses vary in length from two or three words to several hundred words: altogether they total a round two million words.[57] And only 122 contradictions (*contrarietates*) were detected by his successors in all this mass.[58] In addition to his glossing, it was probably Accursius who added to the Corpus, as a tenth

51. *Loc. cit.,* at pages 244 and 245.
52. *Loc. cit.,* at pages 272 and 273.
53. *Loc. cit.,* at pages 268, 269 and 273, note 1.
54. 1 SARTI, at page 146; 5 SAVIGNY, at pages 487 to 495.
55. This notice, except where otherwise specified, is derived from KANTOROWICZ, *Accursio* (1929). "Accursius" seems to be a nickname rather than a name, and of common occurrence but doubtful significance: if so, his real name has been lost.
56. MEIJERS, *Sommes,* at page 243.
57. Seckel laboriously counted 96,260 glosses (without the *Libri Feudorum*) — KANTOROWICZ, *Accursio,* at page 43 — and a random selection of pages gives an average of a little over 20 words to a gloss.
58. Seckel again: KANTOROWICZ, *Accursio,* at page 43. But compare KANTOROWICZ, *Studies* (1938) at page 154, note 29.

"collation" of the Authenticum, the *Libri Feudorum*[59] together with the glosses which James Dove had already given them: Accursius added only a few of his own.

It was apparently the Apparatus on the Code that was finished last,[60] in 1227.[61] He then started again, but only the Institutes[62] received a second rescension, to be dated to 1234:[63] on the rest of the Corpus he did no more than supplement his original rescension. This was perhaps because he was fully occupied with teaching, in the course of which he amassed a great fortune, not all of it honourably. In about 1255 he retired from Bologna, apparently to research quietly in the country house near Florence where he was born; but no second rescension, or any other known result, came out of this. He died early in 1263, aged 78.

Accursius himself had the modesty to leave some points open; but the immense and immediate popularity of his work was due to the number of definitive answers which he furnished. There was now no more to do but to know these; and for a more general view all that was needed was Azzo's Summa on the Code.[64] Accursius' Apparatus

59. The addition is usually attributed to John Bassian, but see MEIJERS, *Sommes,* at page 234, note 84, and *Droit féodal,* at page 263.

60. MEIJERS, *Orléans,* at page 35, note 116, argues from the citations (unspecified) of the apparatus on one member of the corpus in the apparatus on another to an order in which the apparatus on each member was completed; and (although there is no reference) seems to be echoing BIENER, *Geschichte der Novellen* (1824), part ii, s. 292, cited at 5 SAVIGNY 280. But TORELLI, *la Codificazione e la Glossa,* at page 337 (271) has shown that these cross-references are late interpolations.

61. 5 SAVIGNY 281. There is a long discussion on the dating of different parts of the Gloss in 2 NEUMEYER, *die Gemeinrechtliche Entwickelung* (1916), at page 60, note 1 (continuing to page 62). The famous gloss on the first "law" of the Code, which marks the conversion of orthodoxy to the possibility of a conflict of laws, is thought to have been added about 1245: MEIJERS, *Droit international privé* (1934), at page 595. FEENSTRA, *La Glose d'Accurse* (1971), noting that Cino refers to this as an *additio* without saying by whom it was added, would prefer it to have been an interpolation inspired by Odofred.

62. So DIPLOVATATIUS, at page 83. TORELLI, *La Codificazione e la Glossa,* at page 339 (274), points out that even the second rescension was abundantly interpolated, probably in southern France, but mainly from earlier Bolognese glosses which Accursius had seen fit not to produce. See also his *Nuova edizione* (1939-40). All the printed editions from the renaissance down carry the interpolated version. As for a second rescension of the Apparatus on the other members of the corpus also, asserted by MEIJERS, *Orléans,* at page 35, the same note 116, more than one reader has been perplexed by the absence of either argument or authority: now FEENSTRA, *La Glose d'Accurse,* at pages 208 and 222, concludes that Meijers can only have been mistaken. Even Homer nods.

63. 5 SAVIGNY 282. But this dating depends on references to papal decretals; and the argument means nothing until we know how much is interpolated.

64. MEIJERS, *Sommes,* at page 243.

— for the Institutes in the second rescension — became the Standard Gloss:[65] it was customary enough to write it out without the text of the Corpus;[66] but the text was never written without the Apparatus, and before 1627 scarcely an edition was printed without it. His great work was not however immutable. Apart from his own supplementary work there was a continuing process of anonymous interpolation even in the copies officially controlled. The task of restoring the authentic Accursius, the need for which has been often proclaimed, baffles the specialist.[67]

60. Bologna: Examinations and Students. — This is perhaps the point at which to notice that since 1219 serious examination of students had been enjoined on the doctors (by Pope Honorius III) before recommending to the Archdeacon of Bologna the grant of a degree which had always been in his gift. It is unlikely that examinations started only then,[68] but we arrive at certainty with stories of candidates being examined (orally) by Accursius and James Baldwin together.[69] It is not clear that students were bound at this time, as they were later,[70] to five years' of study for a bachelor's degree which entitled them to lecture to a limited extent, and a further three years for a doctorate. In canon law four years were required for a baccalaureat, and a further year for the doctorate; but credit was given for civilian studies, so that a doctorate in both laws could be obtained in ten years.

The doctors were still remunerated — for their teaching, not for the degree — by fees negotiated with the students,[71] usually with each student individually, but sometimes with groups. There is evidently a connection between each student's free choice of a master or masters

65. *Glossa Ordinaria* as usual. There is a legend that an alternative name was *ma. glo.* or *glo. ma.*, extended as *magna glossa* or even as *glossa magistralis* — for example Raphael POWELL, *Glossators,* (1968) 10 Encyclopedia Britannica 489. The abbreviation does in fact occur in references, and does stand for "magna glossa," but this is not collectively the Great Gloss: it means simply the "long gloss" to distinguish the longest of many individual notes on the same "law."
66. The inventory of the goods of James of Belvisio in 1335 (paragraph 105 below) includes a Code and the three Digests, all with Accursius' Apparatus "*ad modum antiquum,*" and also two volumes of the Apparatus by itself on the Old and the New Digests: S. CAPRIOLI, *Giacomo Belvisi,* (1966) 8 D.B.I. 89.
67. FEENSTRA, *La Glose d'Accurse*: Torelli, after a lifetime of articles and "communications," succeeded in editing the Apparatus on the first Book only of the Institutes.
68. 1 RASHDALL 221 and 222; and his editors at pages 231 and 232.
69. MEIJERS, *Orleans,* at page 33. The story is not from Odofred this time, but from another of James' students, Guy of Como who founded the school at Orléans (paragraph 86 below).
70. 1 RASHDALL 220.
71. *Op. cit.,* 208, 209.

and his very general tendency when a doctor himself to record who his master was and to follow him: the choice was made with knowledge of the master's attitude. The students controlled their doctors not only by their individual choice to listen to and pay for their lectures, but also collectively: their *Universitates*, whose president was called *Rector*, regulated and controlled their punctuality and the thoroughness of their coverage, indeed governed the whole of their professional conduct except the granting of degrees.[72]

61. Geoffrey and Bartholomew. — The 1234 *Extravagantes* did not have to wait long for an Apparatus: GEOFFREY of TRANI (*Goffredus de Trano*)[73] provided one about 1240, and between 1241 and 1243 composed also a Summa on them. Geoffrey was one of Azzo's numerous students in civil law, and had taught it briefly at Naples: he had also taught canon law at Bologna. Shortly before his death in 1245 he was made Cardinal[74] by Innocent IV.

At the same time (1245 about) the Standard Gloss to the Decreta was supplemented by BARTHOLOMEW of BRESCIA (*Brixiensis*):[75] his supplements also became standard, and were carried by all editions of the text after John Dutch's glosses. Bartholomew had studied civil law under Hugolin and canon law under Tancred. He taught canon law at Bologna till he was slain in the sack of the city in 1258.

62. Innocent IV. — As Sinibald Fieschi INNOCENT IV[76] had learnt his civil law at the feet of both James Baldwin and Accursius, and counted among his canon-law masters John Dutch and James of Albenga. He does not seem ever to have taught, being made a Cardinal in 1227 and elected to the papacy in 1243. Locked in a life and death struggle with the Emperor Frederick II — it was the death of the Empire, and of the universalistic temporal pretensions of the Papacy too — and also presiding over the Council of Lyon from 1245 to 1251, he nevertheless found time to edit two compilations of his own decretals in 1245 and 1246, and to compose a lengthy COMMENTARY[77] (over 600,000 words) on the 1234 Extravagantes: this was never superseded.

72. *Op. cit.*, 195-197.
73. R. NAZ, (1953) 5 Naz 952.
74. KUTTNER, *der Kardinalat* (1940).
75. G. LE BRAS, (1937) 2 Naz 216.
76. J.A. CANTINI and Ch. LEFEBVRE, (1965) 7 Naz 1029. And compare PIERGIOVANNI, (1967) 14 Studia Gratiana 127.
77. It is not an Apparatus, though usually so called — perhaps because it was the first of the Commentaries, and the Commentary is a development of the Apparatus.

In 1253 he addressed a third compilation, consolidating and adding to the first two, to the Archdeacon of Bologna, and died next year. He is cited as "the Pope" by authors of the next generation, but after that as "Innocent."

Innocent's Commentary was taken up in 1260 and greatly expanded by the admiring but by no means slavish BERNARD of COMPOSTELLA the Younger,[78] but death cut him off in 1267 with only six Titles of the first Book done. It is not known where Bernard studied, and he did not teach: he was in the papal judicial service till preferment took him back to his native Spain. He had been beneficed at Compostella for some time before his death as Archbishop-elect of that see.

63. Bernard of Parma. — A rival Apparatus to the 1234 Extravagantes was prepared by yet another BERNARD, of PARMA this time.[79] At least four rescensions of it are known, dated to 1241, about 1244, about 1252, and between 1263 and his death:[80] the last became the Standard Gloss. This Bernard had studied canon law under Tancred, and taught it at Bologna till his death in 1266. Besides his Apparatus he wrote a Summa, which displaced that of Bernard of Pavia.

64. Hostiensis. — Like Innocent IV, Henry of Susa (*de Segusia*) near Turin was a student of James Baldwin in civil law and of James of Albenga in canon law: he is known by his later cardinalitial title as HOSTIENSIS (of Ostia).[81] Like Innocent again he seems not to have taught, except briefly at Paris where he was Archdeacon in 1239, teaching the Decretals. He began at this stage of his life a Summa on the Decretals, and also what is called a *Lectura* though written by himself. Preferment — he was successively Bishop of Sisteron and Archbishop of Embrun, both then in Provence, from 1244 to 1261, and Cardinal-Bishop of Ostia from 1262 till his death in 1271 — as well as numerous diplomatic missions delayed but did not prevent completion of these works. The Summa (in one and a quarter million words) was published in 1253 and became definitive: like other works of this description it follows the Titles of the text, but unlike them interpolates new Titles where none of the existing ones is appropriate. The *Lectura* was published just before his death, and is a detailed commentary on the text. Pehaps because it totalled two and a half million words,

78. G. BARRACLOUGH, (1934) 49 English Historical Review 487; and again (1937) 2 Naz 777.
79. P. OURLIAC, (1937), 2 Naz 781.
80. KUTTNER, *Glossa Ordinaria* (1945), at page 100.
81. Ch. LEFEBVRE, (1953) 5 Naz 1211.

posterity accorded it less attention. A general characteristic of his work is the insistence, contrary to the more rigid Innocent, on the superiority of canon-law equity over the strict civil law. Although he gives canon law the credit for his equity, he draws for it extensively on the earlier Gosian legists, particularly Placentine.[82]

65. Odofred. — Both systems had now their basic texts, surrounded by standard glosses and endowed with systematic texture by definitive summae. The work might seem to be finished: all that was needed was a historian. ODOFRED,[83] whose master had been James Baldwin, was more of an antiquarian; but without his anecdotes, often enough inaccurate, we should know much less about former times. By 1232 he was in practice in France; in 1238 he was at Padua; and from 1244 in the confidence of Bologna: we may suppose that he started teaching there about that time. Unlike his master he has left us (apart from minor works) Commentaries on both Code and Digest, strictly in the order of the text, in the shape of lectures written by himself in a racy style: a peculiarity is the marking of a new point by *"Or signori"* — "now gentlemen" in Italian. Like his master he was often critical of the orthodox tradition crystallised in Accursius' Standard Gloss. If he rings down the curtain of the first epoch, he is also the precursor of the new, both in his choice of the Commentary as a vehicle and (after a generation's interval in Italy) in his independence. His immediate successors in this independence (as we shall see in Chapter VI) were outside Italy, at Orléans in northern France. He died in 1265.

82. Ch. LEFEBVRE, *Placentinus,* (1965) 7 Naz 1, at columns 6 and 7.
83. 5 SAVIGNY 356-380.

Chapter V

Italian Pause

(1250 - 1315)

Additio, Questio, Disputatio

66. Preliminary. — In Italy and among the "legists" the two generations which follow the death of Accursius are an anticlimax and, being less interesting, are even more obscure. As in the earliest age, the chief work of a law teacher was in the classroom; but instead of scintillating they plodded soberly. Accursius himself had set the fashion of basing his lectures on his largely unexciting Gloss, and this fashion his successors followed, not the example of Odofred. Again as in the earliest days, a teacher's views when he said something more than the Gloss survive in the form of brief notes taken down in the margin of the Gloss, as the Gloss was in the margin of the text. These new ANNOTATIONS — a Gloss upon the Gloss — were called *additiones*. Other literary forms were sparsely cultivated: the details will appear in what follows.

The canonists on the other hand, even in Italy, were not affected in the same dramatic way by Accursius: their science continued to develop on the same lines as before.

67. Guy of Suzzara. — The last fifteen years of Odofred's career saw the rise to prominence of GUY of SUZZARA (*Guido de Suzaria*),[1] a village between Mantua and Reggio: his master is unknown. He is described as "legist" at Mantua in 1247, and doctor of laws there in

1. 5 SAVIGNY 387, supplemented by TORELLI, *Documenti su Guido da Suzzara* (1929).

1250. It must be supposed that he continued to teach there — and that he wrote, if it is true that Odofred cited him[2] — till 1260, when he contracted himself in perpetuity to Modena. During the next ten years there is evidence (which is not conclusive) that he was nevertheless teaching at Padua in 1264 and at Bologna in 1266. It is certain that he attached himself in the latter year to Charles of Anjou (St Louis' younger brother) when that prince, at the behest of two French Popes, took over the Kingdom of Naples from Frederick II's romantic bastard. Manfred was slain in that year, and his nephew and successor Conradin captured two years later: Guy being then on Charles' council gave his legal opinion that Conradin had not incurred the death penalty. It is hardly surprising that this inconvenient advice was disregarded: what is surprising is that the law was even thought relevant. In 1270 Guy hired himself to Reggio, and was living there in 1274, in which year the papal position was further consolidated by a revolution at Bologna exiling the imperialists and establishing the partisans of the papacy. He was called to Bologna for a year in 1279 by the students, to teach the New Digest for 300 lire, and next year arrived at a settlement with Modena of their reciprocal claims. He does not appear again, and (according to a Veronese chronicle) died in 1293.[3]

68. Problems. — Guy left two works which, like his peripatetic career, set the future fashion. One was a set of annotations (*additiones*) to Accursius' standard gloss on all parts of the Corpus Juris.[4] The annotations were often substantial and, to judge from what has been edited, often took the form of Problems (*Questiones*). Guy's other work, much cited by later writers, was a collection of Problems of a peculiar kind, on Local Legislation (*Questiones Statutorum*). Local legislation was peripheric to the general scheme of the law as a whole, and the earlier Bologna legists had paid it scant attention: it had been left to the canonists to deal with the effect of jealously guarded particularism, and that more by way of custom than of "statute." In the new epoch however the field of municipal legislation was extending, mainly in criminal law, but also in succession, marriage and other personal matters, and it was time to deal with it.

69. Disputations. — It became customary to make collections not only of Problems (on legislation or otherwise) resolved by the same

---

2. 1 Sarti 184.
3. But already in 1292 the boundaries of a field are given as the land of Guy of Suzzara "or of his heirs."
4. Torelli, *Sulle orme di Guido da Suzzara* (1935).

teacher, but also (from the middle of the century) of Debated Problems (*Questiones Disputate*) — meaning theses publicly presented and maintained in great detail, not ignoring mere "debating" points, usually by a teacher of some eminence. Such collections were known as Great Books (*Magni Libri*),[5] and included DISPUTATIONS presented by many different teachers. They continued to be compiled and used for teaching till the time of Bartolo in the middle of the next century (paragraph 121 below).

70. Naples. — Charles of Anjou gave new life to the University of Naples, and much good work was produced there, particularly on public law:[6] Naples was one of the few methodically organised governments of the time. But for various reasons little of this influenced the main stream of development: we need mention only two students of Benedict of Isernia, NICOLAS RUFULO, some of whose comments were copied, and JOHN FACCIOLO (*Fazeolus*), born in 1223 at Pisa. The latter was no longer teaching at Naples in 1260, and may have gone to Acre in the Holy Land and written there a Summa on the feudal law in force in the Crusaders' states.[7] In 1278 he appears as city judge at Vicenza.[8]

71. Padua. — The law-school of Padua on the contrary was in the full stream of development. There is no evidence that any school continued to exist there after the early secessions from Bologna;[9] but one was called into existence by the interdict imposed on Bologna in 1260 for its attack on Todi. In 1274, when Bologna was busy with a war with Forlì — and later suffered the revolution already mentioned — the statutes of the Council of Vienne were officially communicated to the University of Padua instead of to Bologna.[10]

72. James of Arena. — If Guy of Suzzara taught at Padua in 1264, it was alongside his student JAMES (*Jacobus*) of ARENA,[11] who had been teaching there since 1261. After teaching at Siena, Bologna and Reggio, James came back about 1286, and about 1287 presented a Disputation the substance of which is recorded by Bartolo on the

5. BELLOMO, *Due Libri Magni* (1969), at pages 256, 257.
6. MEIJERS, *Naples*, at page 165.
7. *Loc. cit.*, at page 158.
8. *Loc. cit.*, at page 159.
9. 2 RASHDALL 14.
10. *Op. cit.*, at page 19.
11. 5 SAVIGNY 399; and see Enrico BESTA, *Riccardo* (1894), at page 11.

conflict of laws.[12] James was teaching at Naples in 1296, the last year in which he is mentioned.

Like his master he composed a collection of Problems on Local Legislation, and annotations (*additiones*) to Accursius' gloss on all three Digests and on the first nine Books of the Code. These annotations were collected, and written out together, but is is far from certain that James himself was responsible for this. At least one manuscript[13] puts his initials after each note, as if they had been extracted one by one from the margins where they were originally written.

73. Others at Padua. — Other early teachers at Padua included the frivolous CERVOTTO,[14] second son of Accursius, who was hired in 1273 at the huge salary of 500 lire: he died in 1287. The canonist JOHN of ANGUISSOLA (*Joannes de Angusellis*)[15] was teaching there in 1275, and left an Apparatus on the 1234 Extravagantes: his master is unknown. Equally unknown is the master of ALBERT GALEOTTI of Parma,[16] mentioned in connection with his native city from 1251 to 1272. It was perhaps only after that that he taught at Padua, and later again at Modena. At Modena he composed, certainly before 1290,[17] a collection of Problems variously known as a *Summa Questionum* or *Margarita* — meaning a pearl, or perhaps rather a string of pearls.

74. Bologna. — At Bologna itself mention may be made in passing of GILLES FOSCARARI (*Aegidius Fuscararius*),[18] the first layman to teach canon law. His *Ordo Judiciarius* dates from about 1260, and he died in 1279.

The revolution of 1274 (paragraph 67 above) brought to the fore two lawyers who had some influence on the future, both with the same first name. ROLANDINO ROMANZI,[19] who was an advocate as well as

12. Translated in (1970) 14 American Journal of Legal History 157, at pages 167 to 170.
13. Madrid National Library, *MS 920, fo. 5r to 9v and 96r to 101r (New Digest).
14. 5 SAVIGNY 323.
15. G. OESTERLE, (1957) 6 Naz 91.
16. 5 SAVIGNY 527.
17. Since it had been incorporated by that date in the *Speculum Judiciale* (paragraph 77 below).
18. 5 SAVIGNY 521. ALIDOSI, at page 68, gives him his doctorate in 1250: the round figure is perhaps a guess.
19. 5 SAVIGNY 556. ALIDOSI, at page 203, dates his doctorate to 1260; but the round figure is suspicious.

a professor, died in 1284; and ROLANDINO PASSAGGERI[20] had been a notary since 1234: he became the chief man in the state, and died as late as 1300. His work on notarial practice (*Summa Artis Notarie*) was celebrated.

75. Francis Accursii. — Accursius and Odofred had been in some sense succeeded by their sons FRANCIS[21] and ALBERT[22] (died in 1300): this would appear to be the factual basis for the wild generalisation that the professorate became hereditary at Bologna at this time.[23] Francis (*Franciscus Accursii*) was his father's student;[24] but in case this may arouse suspicions of nepotism it is to be remarked that Accursius' second and third sons, Cervotto (above) and William (below) received their doctorates at the ages of 19 and 18 in 1259 and 1265, respectively four years (at least) after Accursius' retirement and two years after his death.[25] It is a puzzling fact (on another plane) that, except by going through Francis, it is not possible to establish a personal chain of descent from master to pupil from the earliest days to the latest: the masters of all his contemporaries are unknown.

Francis, notoriously[26] a sodomite (a not uncommon tendency at the time), was enticed away from teaching at Bologna by King Edward I of England in 1273, and remained in English service till 1281. In the interval he and his brothers were sentenced to banishment from Bologna when the revolution of 1274 substituted a pro-papal for a pro-imperial government. Francis resumed his teaching at Bologna in 1282, swearing fidelity to Pope Martin IV, and died in 1293:[27] his father was exhumed to be buried with him in his new tomb.[28]

76. Standard Cases. — Besides teaching, Francis composed *Casus* on the New Digest which became standard and always accompanied his father's standard gloss in the margins of the text. The standard *Casus* composed at the same time on the Code, the Old Digest and

---

20. 5 SAVIGNY 539. ALIDOSI, at page 202, dates his doctorate to 1270. If this is again suspicious, Savigny's date of 1234 (in the text above) strains the credulity.
21. 5 SAVIGNY 306.
22. 5 SAVIGNY 381.
23. 1 RASHDALL 214.
24. KANTOROWICZ, *Accursio* (1929) at page 40. This is on the assumption that the sole evidence, the printed text of Francis' *Casus* on Digest XLVIII.xix.9, §. 16, is not interpolated.
25. *Loc. cit.*, at pages 48 and 39.
26. DANTE, *Inferno*, XV.110.
27. The date of his will: KANTOROWICZ, *Accursio*, at page 194.
28. *Loc. cit.*, at page 60.

the Infortiatum are the work of VIVIAN TOSCHI (*Tuscus*),[29] whose doctorate is dated to 1256. The standard *casus* on the Institutes originated, as we shall see, at Orleans. *Casus* were also composed on the Three Books and on the Authenticum,[30] but they did not become standard.

77. The Speculator. — The one great lawyer of this generation was a Provençal, WILLIAM DURAND.[31] He learnt his canon law at Bologna from Bernard of Parma,[32] and taught it certainly at Modena (at the same time as Guy of Suzzara), perhaps also at Bologna, till about 1267. In this year he entered papal service as *Auditor Generalis,* meaning a judge dealing with appeals to Rome from anywhere in the world. He was a papal governor and military commander from about 1280 to 1291, when he took possession of the bishopric of Mende in Provence — he had been elected five years earlier. In 1294 he refused the archbishopric of Ravenna, but was nevertheless compelled to return to Italy to govern the Romagna: he died at Rome in 1296, and was succeeded at Mende by his nephew of the same name, with whom he is sometimes confused.

It was while he was papal judge that he published his monument, the *Speculum Judiciale* (Mirror of Justice): the nickname SPECULATOR derived from this work supplanted his name in subsequent generations. There was a first edition in 1271 and a second about 1290. The *Speculum* was the culmination of the series of treatises on procedure: its contents were not original — how could they be? — but the excellence of its arrangement made it definitive for the rest of the Middle Ages. The main lines of this arrangement consisted of a division into four Books, on the dramatis personae; procedure proper; criminal procedure; and precedents of pleadings — but also of deeds and including much substantive law. Roffred's *Libelli* were laid under contribution heavily for this last Book, as was Rolandino Passageri on notarial practice, and John White (Jean Leblanc) of Marseilles on testamentary executors (paragraph 55 above). Tancred's influence is naturally everywhere, that of Giles Foscarari considerable. John Facciolo's remarks on summary jurisdiction (*de summariis cognitionibus*) are reproduced;[33] and even the contemporary *Margarita* of Albert

29. 1 SARTI 177; 5 SAVIGNY 339. ALIDOSI, at page 222, gives the Italian form of his surname and the date of his doctorate.
30. 5 SAVIGNY 345.
31. 5 SAVIGNY 539; L. FALLETTI, (1953) 5 Naz 1014.
32. Not Hostiensis, despite the reference to him as "*dominus meus*:" Hostiensis never taught except at Paris in 1239, when William would be 9 years of age or less.
33. Cino (paragraph 108 below) on Code III.i.9 (*judices*), cited by G.M. MONTI, *Cino da Pistoia, Giurista* (1924), at page 169.

Galeotti was incorporated piecemeal "to the last comma." No one was deceived by this, and no one was meant to be: the audience to whom the *Speculum* was addressed was well acquainted with the works drawn upon.

78. Martin Sylliman, Guy of Belvisio. — Half a generation later at Bologna the law was being taught by four doctors whose masters are all unknown. MARTIN SYLLIMAN,[34] the son of a well-known law bookseller, took his degree between 1270 and 1273, and died in 1306. Besides annotations to the standard gloss, a Summa on Feudal Law is attributed to him, largely a copy of that probably written by John Facciolo.[35] This Martin has not infrequently been confused with Martin of Fano (paragraph 58 above.)[36]

GUY of BELVISIO,[37] a canonist, wrote some time in the last third of the century the first general comparative-law treatise, on the Contradictions and Differences between civil and canon law. It is not certain that he was a doctor, but he is said to have been a judge at Bologna. He took the cowl in 1306 and was dead by 1313.

79. Dino. — DINO of MUGELLO[38] was the younger son of a Florentine notary whose surname was Rosoni (*de Rossonibus*). Mugello was a country estate where Dino must have been born; and "Dino" must be a diminutive of something like Rolandino. In 1278, while still a student at Bologna, he paid 195 lire — close on two years of his later professor's stipend — for two canon-law books, Huguccio's Summa on the Decreta and Hostiensis' Apparatus on the Extravagantes. The money may have come from a spell of teaching at Naples: Neapolitan glosses record what seem to be his oral remarks.[39] Despite these books he did not proceed to a canon-law doctorate:[40] by 1279 he was doctor in civil law, and in the same year signed a five-year contract to teach at Pistoia

---

34. 1 SARTI 245 to 247; 5 SAVIGNY 417. ALIDOSI dates his degree to 1266.
35. MEIJERS, *Orléans,* at pages 105, 106.
36. The indulgent reader will correct his copy of (1970) 14 American Journal of Legal History, at page 261, to read "James Buttrigar and Martin Sylliman" on the faith of the same manuscript (*MS Vat. Lat. 2589) as was used for the other corrections of the printed text of Bartolo.
37. Ch. LEFEBVRE, (1953) 5 Naz 1008; Mario CARAVALE, (1966) 8 D.B.I. 96. Cf. ALIDOSI, at page 96.
38. 5 SAVIGNY 447; Roberto BARGIONI, *Dino da Mugello* (Florence, 1920).
39. MEIJERS, *Naples,* at pages 162, 163.
40. The printed edition of his Annotations describes him as *Doctor Utriusque Juris* (Doctor of Both Laws), but in the manuscripts he is simply *Doctor Legum* (i.e. of the civil law). Attempts have been made to show that he was also a canonist, but there is no evidence for it, and his fellow-countryman the canonist John Andrews (paragraph 107 below) expressly says that Dino was no canonist.

on 200 lire a year. He was back in Bologna at the expiry of this period, and in 1289 was salaried by the city at 100 lire, but with liberty to add fees taken from the students in the old way. Dino was "extraordinary" professor, teaching the Infortiatum and New Digest: the Code and the Old Digest were reserved to the "ordinary" professor, who had to be a citizen and was in fact still Francis Accursii. This seems to be the earliest mention of such a division of labour, as it is of a regular state stipend at Bologna.[41] There is a story that Dino one day stood in for Francis and showed his independence by criticising the standard gloss and preferring James Baldwin: Francis when told did the lecture over again, upholding his father, and there was a quarrel.

Dino wrote several treatises, and a fair number of opinions (*consilia*, on cases under litigation) have been preserved: he is the earliest of whom this can be said. But his major surviving work is annotations on the standard gloss of the New Digest and Infortiatum. As in the case of James of Arena, it is not probable that Dino himself composed a collection of these notes, if only because three different versions are known on the New Digest and two on the Infortiatum.[42] The prologue in each case precedes the New Digest, no doubt because lectures started there; and one of these prologues in particular betrays rhetorical leanings. It enquires whether the "cause" of legislation is the orderliness or the disorderliness of human affairs, and eventually finds that orderliness is the "final" cause (the end sought), while disorderliness is the cause in the sense that it necessitates legislation. These no doubt tedious commentaries seem never to have been critically studied, but they are likely to be of great importance historically, as a link in the chain of development from Accursius to Bartolo.

In addition to this complete series of annotations, Dino collected antithetical glosses (*glosse contrarie*), and there are two versions of these contradictions also: one sets out the opposed glosses in pairs and tries to reconcile them by assigning each to different fact-situations,

41. 1 RASHDALL 210. From now on there were two permanent chairs, one in civil law and one in canon law, the first occupant of the latter being the "Archdeacon" (paragraph 82 below).
42. One version of each was printed at the Renaissance. Savigny knew of another (on the New Digest) because Diplovatatius had reported its location in the library of the Spanish College at Bologna, but thought the rest was lost. In fact all three versions of the Annotations on the New Digest exist in manuscript in the Madrid National Library, two in *MS 920, fo. 166 to the end, and the other in *MS 397, fo. 83r to 142v. The Spanish College MS is *272, fo. 91r to 115r. MEIJERS, *Naples*, mentions glosses on the Code in Neapolitan manuscripts.

while the other puts a single fact-situation — a Problem — to which two different solutions result from different glosses.[43]

Dino resisted the blandishments of the King of Naples in 1296 (Bologna doubled his salary); but next year he accepted an invitation to Rome: he took orders and his wife took the veil. Many stories are told about this episode, but it is at least clear that he went to teach civil law in the papal university, the *Curia Romana*: here he composed further annotations to the standard gloss, on the Old Digest. He seems to have died in 1303.

80. The Sext. — It was during Dino's stay in Rome that the official compilation of papal decretals since 1234 was completed: Pope Boniface VIII despatched it in 1298 to the doctors and students of Bologna, Padua and the *Curia Romana,* and also of Orléans and Toulouse (Chapter VI below).[44] This compilation was commonly called the SEXT (*Liber Sextus,* Sixth Book) because the earlier Extravagantes had had five Books, to which this was a supplement; but the Sext, like the Extravagantes, is itself divided into five Books, with the same names and including the same Titles.

There is a last Title, called, like the last Title of the Digest, *de Regulis Juris,* and consisting of a series of maxims, or epigrammatic statements of general principles. It is hardly likely, despite the legend, that Dino composed this Title, but he certainly commented on it; and his view that the *Regulae* were the principles behind all detailed law, which they therefore summed up, was accepted by all later lawyers.[45]

81. William Accursii.[46] — Dino's chair at Bologna passed to WILLIAM, third son of the author of the standard gloss (*Gulielmus Accursii*), but too young to have been his student. William had been doctor of laws since 1265, and composed what are called the Long Cases (*Casus Longi*) on the Institutes: they did not become standard.[47] After his banishment with the rest of his family in 1274 he had taken orders and entered papal service: his return to Bologna lasted only a year, and he died in papal service in 1314.

---

43. BELLOMO, *Glossæ Contrariæ* (1970), at pages 433, 434.
44. 2 FRIEDBERG, *Corpus Juris Canonici,* col. 933-934. Different manuscripts name different lawschools: this is because one was sent to each.
45. Peter STEIN, *Regulæ Juris* (1966), pages 150, 153.
45. 5 SAVIGNY 331.
46. 5 SAVIGNY 331.
47. Except for the prologue and the first three Titles of the first Book: MEIJERS, *Sommes* (1934), at page 237, *Orleans,* at page 31.

82. The Archdeacon. — With GUY of BAISIO[48] we come back to the tradition of doctors whose teachers are known. His family were political exiles from Bologna, and Guy had learnt his law at Reggio — at least that is where he took his canon-law doctorate in 1276. Among his masters was certainly Guy of Suzzara, teaching at Reggio at this time, but perhaps not John of Anguissola (of Padua) despite assertions to that effect. He taught first at Reggio, where he was archdeacon, but by 1283 he had transferred to Bologna (Francis Accursii came back from exile in 1282), and at Bologna in 1295 he became archdeacon again: it is as the ARCHDEACON, and not by name, that later writers cite him. His earliest work, composed at least in part at Reggio, was a collection of Problems (*Questiones*); but his lasting renown depended on the *Rosarium* (rose-garland) published at the beginning of 1300 with the purpose of amplifying and supplementing the standard gloss on the Decreta, corresponding thus for this first compilation to Innocent's commentary on the Extravagantes. It immediately became a text-book kept by the "stationers;" and in 1301 the Archdeacon was given a three-year contract by the city (at 150 lire) to teach the Decreta. He ceased to teach in 1304 and went to Avignon as *auditor* under Pope Clement V, who had transferred the seat of the papacy to this city in Provence (Chapter VI below). But he did not cease to write, and from 1306 to his death was occupied with an Apparatus on the Sext. The virtue both of this work and of his Rosary was the exhaustiveness with which he dealt with his predecessors. He died in 1311 on his way back to Italy.

83. Albert Gandini. — ALBERT GANDINI (*Gandinus, de Gandinis*)[50] of Crema had also learnt his law from Guy of Suzzara, and from John of Anguissola — from the latter explicitly at Padua. Albert did not teach law, but was judge in several towns — Lucca (1281), Bologna (1284), Perugia (1286, 1287), Florence (1288), Bologna again (1289, 1294, 1295), Siena (1299) — and in 1305 mayor of Fermo for a six-month term. We have no later mention of him. While he was at Perugia he wrote a treatise on Criminal Law, which he revised later for publication: he was still working on it at Siena. It deals mainly with procedure and evidence, but also discusses substantive law and many particular problems from his own experience: in its final form

48. LIOTTA, *Guido da Baisio* (1964). This documented account (the documents are at pages 40 to 52) is very different from that of G. MOLLAT, (1953) 5 Naz 1007.
49. Guy had a nephew and a great-nephew of the same name, which sometimes leads to confusion.
50. 5 SAVIGNY 560; KANTOROWICZ, *Gandinus*, Vol. I (1907). Vol. II (1926) is an edition of his treatise, following a discussion of the MS tradition in *Gandinustext*.

it runs to 140,000 words, and its systematic arrangement is admirable. There is also a collection of Problems on Local Legislation (*Questiones Statutorum*), many of them extracted from his treatise, but not all criminal.

84. Lambertin Ramponi; Nicolas Matarello; Bertoluccio. — Finally in this generation three names are remembered for their Disputations. LAMBERTIN RAMPONI (*de Ramponibus*)[51] took his doctorate in 1269, and after teaching at Bologna died in 1304. NICOLAS MATARELLI[52] is styled doctor of laws at Modena in 1270, and teaching law there for at least some time before his exile in 1284, probably as an opponent of the domination of Azzo di Este. Fame came to him as professor at Padua, probably enough from 1284 to his death shortly after 1310, except for a brief recall to Modena in 1306 on Azzo's downfall, to be "Defender of the People's Liberty." Besides Disputations[53] he abridged Odofred's Commentaries on both Code and Digest. The third name is BERTOLUCCIO PRETI, who took his doctorate at Bologna in 1295, and died in 1318.[54] One of his Disputations which has survived in outline[55] (on the construction of a will) notices first the ultramontane (French) view, which he characterises as equitable because it gave effect to the testator's probable intention; but he concludes against it in application of the texts of the law. He is said to have left also annotations on the Digest and on the Code, and Problems much cited in the next generation.

We must now break off to trace the development of this "ultramontane" approach, which which was beginning to trouble Italian spirits.

---

51. 5 SAVIGNY, 426. ALIDOSI, at page 154, has two of this name, one who became doctor in 1254 and died in 1269, the other who became doctor in 1276 and died in 1304.
52. 5 SAVIGNY 430; E.P. VICINI, *Di Niccolò Matarelli: Ricerche e Critica* (1900). His father's nickname was *Matarellus,* and it was only later in his career that Nicholas is styled *"de Matarellis."* There is no evidence for assertions that he taught at Bologna or at Pisa.
53. One of these is recorded by several later writers, including (briefly) Bartolo, translated in (1970) 14 American Journal of Legal History, at page 271. He is credited with comment on the first nine Books of the Code and on all three Digests; but one may guess that this is the same work as his abridgment.
54. ALIDOSI, at page 41.
55. It is summarised by John Andrews (paragraph 107 below) in his commentary on Sext III.xi.1 (c. *si pater, de Testamentis*), his §§ 20 and 21 as edited.

Chapter VI

French Interlude

(1240 - 1315)

Repetitio, Lectura Reportata

85. Orléans. — If the suppression of Roman-law teaching in England was definitive,[1] its suppression in France in 1219 was not. It was in any case applicable only to Paris; and courses in civil law were already being given at Angers and Orléans by 1235,[2] when Pope Gregory IX issued a reminder of the limited nature of the ban. Both were schools of higher education specifically for the clergy — this in strong contrast with the Italian schools — and both taught also canon law. Something is known of Angers;[3] but only Orléans was of significance for the future.

86. Guy of Como. — One looks in vain for any trace at Orléans of continuity with the suppressed school at Paris: it was a new departure, and the earliest known professor was a Lombard, Guy of Como.[4] He was an elder contemporary of his homonym Guy of Suzzara with whom the last chapter opened, having sat at the feet of Hubert of Bobbio and also (at Bologna) of James Baldwin. He had taken his doctorate by

---

1. Bracton, writing within twenty years of the suppression, seems not to have attended any school of civil law, though this a matter of dispute between the experts. His knowledge of Roman law seems to have come from reading by himself, particularly Azzo's Summa on the Institutes. The Roman-law doctrines which he imported from this reading lay long dormant, but had much influence on English law in the eighteenth century: T.F.T. Plucknett, *Concise History of the Common Law* (5th edition, 1956), at pages 261, 262.
2. Meijers, *Orléans,* at page 28.
3. *Loc. cit.,* page 6, note 3.
4. *Loc. cit.,* pages 30 to 35, corrected by Feenstra, *Guido de Cumis* (1968-1969).

at least 1234 (since James Baldwin took part in the examination); was teaching at Orléans by 1243; and survived till at least 1263. While there he annotated Accursius's standard gloss on the Old Digest and on the Code and composed Studies (perhaps the best translation of *Repetitiones*) and Problems (*Questiones de Facto*) on various "laws" of the Old Digest, all on matters of procedure. We also owe to him the standard *Casus* on the Institutes, taken down by students who described him in the third person (this was to be typical of Orléans) when he put them in the course of his lectures.[5]

87. Other Early Teachers at Orléans. — The next (but overlapping) generation of teachers were all French. Two of them however, PETER of AUXONNE (*de Ausona*)[6] in Burgundy, and SIMON of PARIS (*de Parisius* — sic),[7] had taken their doctorates at Bologna[8] — their masters are unknown. Even the place of study of JOHN of MONCHY (*de Monciaco*),[9] FULK of LAON (*de Loduno*)[10] and the shadowy GUICHARD of LANGRES (*Lingonensis*)[11] is unknown. Of these five Peter and Fulk left no writings, but Peter left his books to the Sorbonne, and this legacy was the beginning of its library. Simon of Paris, besides a treatise on procedure, wrote Studies and Problems, and also glosses. Guichard and John left only glosses.

88. Glossa Aurelianensis. — There was no complete Apparatus in use specially at Orléans:[12] contemptuous Italian references to an "Orléans gloss" are in the sense of single comments on individual passages. And the contempt was largely a reaction to the lack of reverence at Orléans for Accursius[13] — a liberty which was due in turn partly to the rhetorical inclinations of clerics who were all Masters of Arts before they embarked on law,[14] and partly no doubt to the earliest professor, Guy of Como, having studied under James Baldwin. An oddly

5. There are two versions in respect of the second part of the Institutes (III.xiii to the end), no doubt due to different students having been at work. The printed edition is from a manuscript which lacked the first few leaves: they were supplied from the *Casus* of William Accursii (paragraph 80 above) — FEENSTRA, *loc. cit.*, pages 240 to 243.
6. MEIJERS, *Orléans,* at page 43.
7. *Loc. cit.,* at pages 36 to 38.
8. *Loc. cit.,* at page 29.
9. *Loc. cit.,* at pages 39 to 42.
10. *Loc. cit.,* at page 44.
11. *Loc. cit.,* at page 52.
12. *Loc. cit.,* at page 55.
13. *Loc. cit.,* at pages 111, 113, 119.
14. *Loc. cit.,* at page 114.

juvenile attitude at Orléans was the civilians' profession of contempt for the canonists.[15]

89. Clerici Regis. — Men to whom the study of Roman law had given the power of precise analysis of particular circumstances were much in demand in the French royal administration — *Curia Regis* as in England. They were there styled King's Clerks (*Clerici Regis*).[16] A Bolognese glossator, Lothar of Cremona, had held such an appointment as early as 1202; and after 1226 two ex-professors from Paris were so employed. A close connection with Orléans and its new school was established by the King's Clerks Stephen of Montfort and Odo of Lorris.[17] Stephen (died in 1269) was Dean of St Aignan at Orléans; and Odo was there from 1252. In 1260 he became Bishop of Bayeux, and surrounded himself with cleric legists from Orléans.

The useful practical service, in or out of the *Curia Regis*, which would merit a mitre[18] required an ability to adapt to the context, part of which comprised vigorously defended local customary laws. In the eyes of both professors and students the significance of legal studies was at least partly the plum at the end of the road;[19] and this school was therefore attuned to local custom[20] to a degree which to Bologna had seemed unworthy. Apart from continual references in passing we find two careless compilations of customary law under the influence of Orléans before 1260:[21] *les Etablissements de St Louis*, and *Li Livres de Jostice et de Plet*.

90. Resignations in 1260. — The afflux of students to Orléans led to a housing problem; but the students — perhaps because they were churchmen — did not band together as at Bologna to deal with this. It was the professors who bound themselves by oath not to teach unless they were given power to control rents. They were given this power, but it was withdrawn, and in about 1260 they all resigned.[22] Peter of Auxonne took service with the King of England, and Fulk of Laon with the King of France. Simon of Paris took the opportunity to add canon law to his qualifications, and in 1268 he too took service with the King

15. *Loc. cit.*, at page 113.
16. *Loc. cit.*, at pages 8 to 10.
17. *Loc. cit.*, at pages 12 to 15.
18. *Loc. cit.*, at page 20.
19. *Loc. cit.*, at pages 25 to 27, 114.
20. *Loc. cit.*, at pages 23, 24.
21. *Loc. cit.*, at pages 56 and 57.
22. *Loc. cit.*, at page 36. It is not certain that Guichard was with them: he may have been dead already.

of France as King's Clerk. John of Monchy is last mentioned in 1265, after having been involved with Charles of Anjou before he went to Naples (paragraph 67 above). Once established at Naples in 1268 Charles filled all posts with Frenchmen.[23] His first Chancellor (till 1271) was a former Orléans law-student;[24] and in 1272 he appointed Simon of Paris Chancellor and also Rector of the revived University of Naples. But Simon died the next year.

91. Peter Peregrossi. — The resignation of all the professors in 1260 or so did not bring the law-school to an end. Another Lombard, PETER PEREGROSSI (*Petrus de Petris Grossis,* "Greatstones")[25] of Milan began to teach about then or even earlier, having learnt his law from Odofred. He left a preface to the Digest derived from Odofred's, a commentary on the attachment of a reluctant defendant's property, and the beginning of a course on the Institutes which is dated to 1260. He obtained ecclesiastical preferment before 1273, was created Cardinal in 1282, and died in 1295.

92. James of Révigny. — Greater than him, and by his originality constituting a new departure in the study of Roman law, was a native product, JAMES of REVIGNY (*de Raveniaco,* or to the Italians later *de Ravanis*) in Lorraine.[26] He had learnt his law at Orléans at the feet of John of Monchy (chiefly), Guichard of Langres and Simon of Paris.[27] He left[28] courses (*lecture*) on the Code (perhaps soon after 1265), on the Institutes (soon after 1270), on the Old Digest (before 1273), and also on the Infortiatum (lost), the New Digest and the Authenticum.[29] The course on the Code alone is a little over a million words. His last work was the first of a long line of legal dictionaries, discussing key words in alphabetical order. It is noteworthy for its citation of pre-Accursian Bolognese jurists.[30]

23. *Loc. cit.,* at page 24.
24. *Loc. cit.,* at page 55.
25. *Loc. cit.,* at pages 46 to 52.
26. *Loc. cit.,* at pages 60, 61.
27. *Loc. cit.,* at pages 61, 62. The received opinion that he was a student of James Baldwin or of Roffred is due to misreading the texts, and is chronologically impossible: *ibid.,* pages 59, 60.
28. *Loc. cit.,* pages 71 to 78.
29. He has had the misfortune to have his courses on the Institutes and on the Code printed at the Renaissance under the names respectively of Bartolo and of Peter of Belleperche (paragraph 121 and 95 below): the latter was reprinted photographically in 1968 with no indication that the attribution to Peter of Belleperche is erroneous. See MEIJERS, *loc. cit.,* pages 68 and 74.
30. Giuliana D'AMELIO, *Il Dictionarium Juris de Jacques de Révigny,* (1972) 40 Tijdschrift 43. See for the chronology pages 56 and 57, note 39.

James had accepted preferment by 1280.[31] He was elected Bishop of Verdun in 1289, and died on his way to Rome in 1296 in search of a solution to his perennial quarrels with the inhabitants: this was the same year as the death of the Speculator and the last mention of James of Arena (paragraphs 77 and 72 above).

93. Lecture and Repetitiones. — These courses were lecture-notes, taken down by a trusted student (*reportator*) and settled with the master: James himself is not "I" but "my master."[32] A senior professor would take a two-year cycle,[33] expounding in one year the Old Digest and in the other the Code, and in the same two years dealing with some of the New Digest and some of the Infortiatum; but he would supplement these courses with STUDIES (*repetitiones*) in greater depth, delivered at the end of each semester on selected "laws" as texts. The lecture notes were compiled with the Studies inserted at the place of these selected laws; and since the Studies were often different the next time round, successive rescensions of the courses might differ in the Studies included. It was also fashionable to make separate compilations of these Studies, not always confined to those of a single teacher.

The students were free to choose their professor, and in the early days when the numbers of the teaching staff were not limited (paragraph 94 below) the fittest (at least from the students' point of view) survived. Visiting professors were frequent and popular: one of them was Accursius' son Francis in 1274 (then in the service of the King of England), and it is said that James of Révigny disguised himself as a student to debate with him.[34]

94. Students of James of Révigny. — Several of James' students taught alongside him, and three of them left at about the same time as he did. JAMES of BOULOGNE (*de Bolonia*),[35] who left Studies and Problems, went to the bench as judge in the Parlement of Paris, and died in 1301. RALPH of HARCOURT (*Radulfus de Haricuria*)[36] wrote a treatise on Actions (a commentary on that Book of the Institutes), and with his brother Robert (also a student under James of Révigny, but never a professor) founded the Collège de Harcourt at Paris in

31. MEIJERS, *Orléans,* page 63.
32. *Loc. cit.,* pages 64, 65.
33. *Loc. cit.,* pages 65, 66.
34. *Loc. cit.,* page 59.
35. *Loc. cit.,* pages 84, 85.
36. *Loc. cit.,* pages 85, 87, 88.

1280: he died in 1307. Another of James' students, PETER of LACHAPELLE (*de Capella*)[37] was already teaching in 1270 and may have gone on till 1287. He was in royal service from that date and so remained (despite papal appointment in 1291 to the see of Carcassonne) till his translation in 1298 to Toulouse. He died in 1312. The third of those who left about 1280 was PETER of MORNAY,[38] but he came back to Orléans as Bishop in 1288. The government of the law-school belonged to the bishop, and it was Peter who limited the number of senior professors to five. He was translated to Auxerre in 1296, and for the last two years of his life (1304 to 1306) was also Chancellor of France.

95. Peter of Belleperche. — The second Orléans teacher to make a permanent mark was PETER of BELLEPERCHE (*de Bella Pertica*),[39] who began to teach just when James of Révigny stopped. He had learnt his law at Orléans, and while James was teaching, but not from James — another currently received error. His master was Ralph of Harcourt, and his frequent citation of James is always from his written works, not from his oral teaching. Peter's courses (*lecture*) on the Title of the Institutes dealing with Actions (before 1282) and others on four Titles of the New Digest and on the first eight Books of the Code have come down to us;[40] but his major work consisted of numerous Studies (*repetitiones*) on the Code, the New Digest and the Old Digest, and of Distinctions (called *Brocarda* or *Questiones Auree*, golden problems) numbering between five and six hundred.[41] Peter left Orléans for royal service about 1296 — but he gave a visiting lecture at Bologna in 1300.[42] Ten years later (1306) he succeeded Peter of Mornay as Bishop of Auxerre and as Chancellor of France, but like him occupied the latter post for two years only, dying in 1308.

Law continued to be competently taught at Orléans after Peter left, by his student LAMBERT of SALINS[43] and others, for at least another century; but only James of Revigny and Peter of Belleperche influenced the later development of the law, by the attention paid to their writings in Italy, as we are about to see.

---

37. *Loc. cit.*, pages 88, 89.
38. *Loc. cit.*, pages 81 to 83.
39. *Loc. cit.*, pages 95 to 98.
40. *Loc. cit.*, pages 99 to 103.
41. *Loc. cit.*, page 102.
42. He did not, as is sometimes alleged, write a treatise on feudal law plagiarising Martin Sylliman (paragraph 78 above): *loc. cit.*, page 104.
43. *Loc. cit.*, pages 106 to 108.

96. Coutumes. — In the second generation at Orléans, as in the first, the teachers of law refer to local custom, but none of them wrote a treatise on it, or even, as in Italy with the "statutes," made collections of problems arising out of it. Some works on custom appeared, written by men trained in Roman law and at the law-schools, but the authors were not teachers. The great name in this small band is Philip de Beaumanoir,[44] judge at Clermont-en-Beauvaisis whose custom he described in French about 1280: he died about 1296. Beaumanoir did not denature custom; but his description of it was Romanist, as was his supplementing of it. With him the Customs clearly entered into the legal family.

97. Southern France. — In southern France legal instruction is not known to have continued at Montpellier after Placentine's death.[45] Toulouse was made a *Studium Generale* by bull of Pope Gregory IX as early as 1229;[46] but no one studied law there before 1280.[47] Many southern Frenchmen studied law in Italy, and returned to practise and sometimes to write — John White (Jean Leblanc) of Marseilles about 1260 has already been mentioned (paragraph 55 above). Now and again, on an individual basis, they taught law on their return: canon law for example was taught by PETER of SAMSON[48] at Avignon after study at Turin and teaching at Bologna from 1246 to 1250; and civil law was taught by another BASSIAN[49] who had studied under Accursius and glossed his Apparatus. He was at Orange in 1268, and that is probably where he taught.

98. Abbas Antiquus. — Peter[50] had come back to France in 1252 for the specific purpose of drafting a Rule of clerical conduct for the archdiocese of Nîmes: he also left a *lectura* on the Extravagantes. A notable student of his, who similarly wrote a *lectura* on the Extravagantes and another on the later constitutions of Innocent IV, was BERNARD of MONTMIRAT.[51] Bernard taught canon law at Béziers, and

44. Fr. OLIVIER-MARTIN, *Histoire du Droit français* (1951), no. 83, at page 117.
45. MEIJERS, *Toulouse* (1938), at page 169.
46. 1 RASHDALL 8.
47. MEIJERS, *Toulouse,* at page 174.
48. His master is unknown. MEIJERS, *Toulouse,* at page 172, shows that it was not James of Albenga; and still less — if for reasons merely chronological — was it John of Faenza, as R. NAZ asserts in (1957) 6 Naz 1497.
49. MEIJERS, *Toulouse,* at page 171.
50. R. NAZ, (1957) 6 Naz 1497.
51. This personal name was identified with the person bearing the epithet of "Abbas Antiquus" independently by KUTTNER, *Wer war...* (1937), and by MEIJERS, *Toulouse* at pages 172, 173.

was then from 1266 to 1286 Abbot of Montmajour. Appointed Bishop of Tripoli but swiftly expelled by the Saracens, he died in 1296 as administrator of the monastery of Monte Cassino. Later writers referred to him as the ABBOT — or as the Elder Abbot (*Abbas Antiquus*) to distinguish him from a younger writer of the same dignity whom we shall meet later (paragraph 141 below).

99. Toulouse and Montpellier. — Soon after 1280[52] there was a regular law-school at TOULOUSE, purely clerical as at Orléans; and at about the same time another at Montpellier.[53] At Montpellier the teachers were laymen: King Philip the Fair's counsellor William de Nogaret taught there from 1287. Turnover was very rapid, and many names are known, but we can select only a few, all from Toulouse. WILLIAM FERRERS (*de Ferreriis,* de Ferrières),[54] who seems to have learnt his law from Peter Peregrossi at Orléans, was teaching at Toulouse by 1284. He wrote glosses to all parts of the Corpus Juris, a treatise on pleading, and another on custom in general. 1289 saw him in papal service, 1290 with the Neapolitan Angevins, 1294 a Cardinal: he died in 1295. PETER FERRERS[55] (his connection with William is not known) taught at Toulouse from 1288 to 1294, and died in 1308: he annotated the standard gloss.

100. Avignon, the Clementines. — Bernard de Got, Archbishop of Bordeaux and formerly student of Peter of la Chapelle at Orléans, was crowned Pope at Lyon in 1305 as Clement V. He raised Orléans to the rank of a *Studium Generale,* and made a cardinal of his former master, then Bishop of Toulouse.[56] Clement V never left France: in 1309 he made his fateful decision to fix the seat of the papacy at Avignon. He was succeeded in 1316 by Jacques Duèse[57] who had also learnt his law at Orléans and who, as John XXII, issued a compilation of Clement's decretals in 1317. The CLEMENTINES, as they were called, were arranged in the same way as previous compilations: no more official compilations were made, though decretals continued to issue. The Avignon papes showered favours on the French law-

52. MEIJERS, *Toulouse,* at page 174.
53. A. GOURON, *Les juristes de l'école de Montpellier,* (1970) Ius Romanum Medii Aevi, IV.3a, at page 12. This is a detailed study of the Montpellier law-school, bringing out its peculiar status as politically dependant more on the crown of Majorca (and later of Aragon) than on that of France.
54. MEIJERS, *Toulouse,* at page 175.
55. *Loc. cit.,* at page 178.
56. MEIJERS, *Orléans,* at page 88.
57. MEIJERS, *Toulouse,* page 174, note 41.

schools,[58] particularly Toulouse and Montpellier; but (to anticipate) they withered when this stimulus disappeared.

101. William of Cunh. — It was at this time that WILLIAM of CUNH[59] (in the parish of Rabastens, near Toulouse) was teaching at Toulouse, where he had probably studied, perhaps under Peter Ferrers. He annotated the standard gloss on all parts of the Corpus Juris except the Institutes; but his influential work consisted of *lecturae* in the Orléans style (but much shorter because eclectic) on the Old Digest and the Code, taken down by a regrettably muddled "reporter." The former course was delivered in 1315-1316, and the latter in 1316-1317. He had to delegate to an assistant some of his lectures in the last year while he was acting as judge of civil appeals in the absence of the incumbent on diplomatic business. In 1320 he was appointed Bishop of Bazas, in 1325 of Comminges: he died at the beginning of 1336.

102. William of Montlezun. — The canonist WILLIAM of MONTLEZUN (*de Montelauduno*)[60] had learnt his law at Paris, and taught it at Toulouse up to 1314. He was present at Clement V's coronation at Lyon in 1305, and between then and 1316 composed a course (*lectura*) on the Sext. In 1319 he published a commentary (called an Apparatus) on the new Clementines, together with three of John XXII's subsequent decretals: the part on these decretals had a durable reputation; but the rest of his writings were eclipsed by John Andrews (paragraph 107 below). William was appointed Abbot of Montierneuf at Poitiers in 1321, and so remained till his death in 1343.

103. John Faure. — Contemporary with these was JOHN FAURE[61] (*Joannes Faber*, in English "Smith") de Montbroud in the Angoumois, called also de Roussines (*de Runcinis*) from the fief which came to him from his mother, his elder brother taking their father's. He learnt

58. *Loc. cit.*, at page 183.
59. "*de Cuniho*" in documents; "*de Cugno*" in Toulouse manuscripts referring to him as a teacher; "*de Cuneo*" (usually) in Italy. See B. BRANDI, *Notizie intorno a Guillelmus de Cunio* (1892); P. FOURNIER, *Gu. Cu.* (1921); MEIJERS, *Orléans* at page 123, and *Toulouse*, pages 186 to 188; H. GILLES, *Trois consultations des doctores Tholosani*, (1971) 39 Tijdschrift 157, at pages 217, 218.
60. P. FOURNIER, *Montlauzun* (1921), is still best account. See also G. MOLLAT, (1953) 5 Naz 1078.
61. P. FOURNIER, *Jean Faure* (1921). His sister was already widowed when their parents made a settlement of their property in 1284. See also MEIJERS, *Toulouse*, at page 208.

his law at Montpellier, but does not name his teachers: perhaps they were among the dialectical "windbags" for whom his keen mind had no patience. He practised with profit at Angoulême, and was for thirteen (unspecified) years an itinerant judge exercising seigneurial jurisdiction. During this period he wrote his Manual (*Breviarium*) on the Code, perhaps between 1325 and 1330. His commentary on the Institutes was later than 1335; and he perhaps died about 1340. These works are not courses, but true commentaries in the style of the canonists. He cites all his predecessors, but his favourite authorities are James of Révigny and Peter of Belleperche. His writings became known latter in Italy,[62] and in France they enjoyed a very high authority, partly because they are both concise and comprehensive, partly because they not only take account of local custom but absorb it: even feudal tenures are fitted into Roman-law categories.

104. Henri Bohic. — Perhaps not much younger, though his written work is a generation later than that of William of Cunh, is the Breton HENRY BOHIC.[63] He learnt his civil law at Orléans and his canon law at Paris, where for the rest of his life he lectured on the 1234 Extravagantes. His work is entitled "Distinctions," but it is a commentary on this compilation, finished in 1349. The arrangement of his ideas is so little methodical that he thought it necessary to append a systematic index in that year. He cites all his predecessors, including very frequently William of Montlezun, but not forgetting the Italians, down to John Andrews among the canonists and Cino (paragraph 108 below) among the legists. With him an epoch closes in France; and we have run ahead of the Italian story, to which we must now return.

---

62. Fifty years later, by the accident that Paul of Castro (paragraph 134 below) taught at Avignon and came to know of them: MEIJERS, *Orléans*, at page 114.
63. P. FOURNIER, *Bohic* (1938). All previous accounts, including that of A. LAMBERT, (1937) 2 Naz 927, are chronologically misleading.

Chapter VII

Maturity

(1300 - 1360)

The Commentary

105. James of Belvisio. — James of Belvisio (*Jacobus de Bellovisu*)[1] was the son of the canonist Guy above. He learnt his law at Bologna under Francis Accursii and Dino, and was teaching there as a "bachelor" in 1296 and 1297. Prevented by political intrigue[2] from obtaining his doctorate there, he attached himself to Charles II of Anjou, King of Naples and Count of Provence, and early in 1298 received his doctorate in the King's presence at Aix-en-Provence from the Chancellor of the University of Naples: he taught at Naples till 1304. From at least 1308[3] to 1321 (with intervals) he was teaching at Perugia: Perugia[4] had been a centre of higher studies since 1285, including law from 1296. Pope Clement V, having been elected there in 1305, granted the school (from Avignon in 1308) the privileges of a *Studium Generale*, and in 1318 Pope John XXII specified the right to create doctors in both laws to be recognised everywhere.

---

1. 6 Savigny 60; S. Caprioli, (1966) 8 D.B.I. 89, fixing his birth in 1270 or later.
2. The college of doctors consistently refused, from 1292 to 1304, to present relatives of members of the faculty. This praiseworthy reaction to accusations of making the doctorate hereditary (paragraph 75 above) seems to have had the effect of excluding any citizen (not foreigners), and civic clamour eventually forced its abandonment.
3. He was two years at Bologna (1304-1306), but convulsions crowned by an interdict sent him on his travels again. From 1306 et 1308 he is said to have been at Padua; and a story that he was at Siena with Oldrad (paragraph 114 below) and from jealousy procured the latter's expulsion may, if true, have to be accommodated here. In 1309 he was at Bologna again, and between 1311 and 1321 Bologna continually tried to get him back. He was possibly absent at Naples again for part of this period.
4. Ermini, *Perugia,* (1971), pages 18 to 29.

All this time Bologna had been trying to get James back: as a Bolognese citizen he had property there liable to confiscation, and it took dexterity on his part, combined with diplomatic representation by Perugia, to ward off the threat. In 1321 the situation became critical: a Spanish student was condemned to death at Bologna, and summarily executed, for an attempt to abduct with armed force a notary's daughter.[5] The great majority of the student body, indignant at so savage a reaction to a natural prank, seceded to Imola with at least three prominent foreign doctors (paragraph 109 below). To replace them Bologna increased its pressure on James, and he had to yield: once back he stayed there till his death in 1335.

He left comments on the Authenticum and on the *Libri Feudorum;* a treatise on criminal procedure (*Practica Criminalis*); and annotations to the standard gloss on the Old Digest.

106. James Buttrigar. — In contrast to the itinerant James of Belvisio, two of Martin Sylliman's students, both Bolognese citizens, were teaching continuously at Bologna from the beginning of the century till both succumbed to the Black Death in 1348. The legist JAMES BUTTRIGAR[6] had the same difficulty as James of Belvisio in attaining to the rank of doctor, but did not leave Bologna. He was a notary from 1293, and then taught as a "bachelor" in 1307 and 1308, between two visits of the other James. In 1309 he acquired his doctorate. At the secession of 1321 (above) he went after the students and brought their terms back to the civic authorities at Bologna; but a year elapsed before they were accepted and most of the students returned. Remarkable more for the solidity than for the brilliance of his intellect, he left *lecture* on the Code and the Old *Digest,* as well as Problems (*questiones*) and Disputations.

107. John Andrews. — Martin's other student, JOHN ANDREWS[7] (*Joannes Andree* — son of Andrew), born like Dino in the valley of Mugello near Florence, was one of the two outstanding figures of this

5. This episode has been much misrepresented. For the sober facts, with their political undercurrents, see F. FILIPPINI, *l'Esodo degli studenti da Bologna nel 1321,* (1921) 6 Studi e Memorie per la Storia dell' Università di Bologna, pages 107 to 157.
6. 6 SAVIGNY 68; A. Tognoni CAMPITELLI, (1971) 13 D.B.I. 498. That he was Martin's student is demonstrated by MEIJERS, *Orléans,* at page 117. Meijers also shows (at page 116) that the view that he studied under Peter of Belleperche is due to the omission of a word in a manuscript.
7. 6 SAVIGNY 98; S. STELLING-MICHAUD, (1957) 6 Naz 89. See also KUTTNER, *Johannes Andreae* (*Extravagantes*) (1963).

generation. His canon-law master was the Archdeacon, Guy of Baisio,[8] and he took his canon-law doctorate between 1296 and 1300. By 1305 he had already provided the Sext with an Apparatus which became its standard gloss. Twenty years later he did the same for the Clementines.[9] Less to his credit is the recast in 1317 of the University statutes, the chief change being that they were greatly lengthened by the addition of much detail.[10] Between 1336 and 1342 he annotated his own Apparatus on the Sext; composed his Wednesday Problems (*Questiones Mercuriales,* a quarter of a million words) on its last Title, the *Regulae Juris;* and wrote commentaries called *Novella* (after his mother and daugther) on both the 1234 Extravagantes and the Sext without its last Title (respectively over one and a half million words and nearly half a million words). For the latter he drew widely on the commentaries of his master the Archdeacon and of William of Montlezun. He wrote no commentary on the Clementines, but he annotated copiously his own Apparatus, citing the *Lectura* of his student Paul Lazzari (paragraph 109 below):[11] it may be that he thought Paul's work adequate as a commentary. Finally, between 1346 and 1347 (he died in 1348), he annotated William Durand's Speculum: his annotations have the character of a complete Apparatus, and acquired all the prestige of a standard gloss, in the sense that in future the Speculum always carried it. Apart from his wide learning, John's historical sense of the relation between his predecessors gives great value to his work.

108. Cino to 1321. — If the learned John Andrews was master of the past, the future lay with the other great name of this very numerous generation, the unconventional CINO Sinibuldi, of PISTOIA (*de Pistorio, Pistoriensis*):[12] his personal name is the last half of "Guittoncino."

---

8. He also listened when very young to Giles Foscarari, who died in 1289. And he is given as an additional civil-law master Richard Malombra (paragraphs 112, 113 below): the authority is of doubtful authenticity, and chronological considerations make it practically impossible.
9. A minor canonist at this time (about 1320) was LAPO, ABBOT of SAN MINIATO. — F. RUBOD, (1957) 6 Naz 344. All three members of this designation lend themselves to confusion with other teachers: Lapo of Castiglionchio (paragraph 133 below); the Elder and the Sicilian Abbots (paragraphs 98 above and 141 below) and Ricovero of San Miniato (paragraph 109 below). It is not clear where Lapo taught, but he left *lecture* on the Sext and on the Clementines, and annotated a treatise by Frederick Petrucci (paragraph 109 below).
10. 1 RASHDALL 173, 174.
11. KUTTNER, *Johannes Andreæ* (*Clementines*) (1965).
12. 6 SAVIGNY 72. Cino has attracted several special studies, the most thorough being by Luigi CHIAPPELLI, *Vita e opere giuridiche di Cino da Pistoia* (1881), supplemented by *Nuove ricerche su Cino da Pistoia* (1911). Of some value also are G. ZACCAGNINI, *Cino da Pistoia* (1919), and G.M. MONTI, *Cino da Pistoia, giurista* (1924).

He must have known Dino while the latter was teaching at Pistoia (1279 to 1284), but it is not probable that he was taught by him there: certain it is that Dino was his master at Bologna, as were Francis Accursii and Lambertin Ramponi. Cino was at Bologna from at least 1292 to 1302, as a student and probably also teaching, and it is likely enough that his *Glosse Contrarie,* following in Dino's footsteps, were composed at this time.[13] In 1302 he went back to Pistoia, but was banished next year for being a nobleman of the wrong party, till the next turn of the wheel brought him back in 1306. He was then briefly judge, but the determination of the victors to consolidate their vengeance through the courts led to his resignation. Poet as well as lawyer, he was the friend and admired friend of Dante: both had suffered (as had many others) from the perpetual personal persecution of party strife in the Italian cities, and both longed for a superior authority to put an end to it. This authority both saw in the German Emperor, Henry VII of Luxemburg, to whose suite Cino attached himself on his arrival in Italy in 1310: he acted as judge in the imperial court set up at Rome. Both realised that with Henry's death in 1313 the dream was shattered, but neither that it was beyond recall.

In 1314 Cino published his great Commentary on the first nine Books of the Code, much of which had evidently been composed many years earlier; and at the end of the same year he at last took his doctorate at Bologna. But he does not seem yet to have settled down to teaching: in the next few years he was probably in lucrative practice at the bar. He was on missions in the March of Ancona in 1320 and 1321, and the evil odour of papal administration there (from Avignon) never afterwards left his nostrils.

109. Siena and Perugia. — The secession of 1321 (paragraph 105 above) was initially to Imola, whence students and professors received pressing invitations from SIENA, Perugia[14] and Padua.[15] Siena prevailed, having been both the quickest off the mark and the most generous in its terms. Most of the students went back to Bologna in the following year, but the professors stayed longer, their absence from Bologna being compensated to some extent by the reverse transfer of James of Belvisio (above) from Perugia to Bologna. Two hundred gold florins a year had secured the services of Cino as professor at Siena; and with him were engaged three canonists of a certain reputation, all students

---

13. BELLOMO, *Glossæ Contrariæ* (1970), at pages 435 to 439.
14. 2 RASHDALL 33 and 41.
15. 2 RASHDALL 16.

of John Andrews above. These were FREDERICK PETRUCCI,[16] himself of Siena; RICOVERO (*Recuperus*) of SAN MINIATO (under Pisa);[17] and PAUL LAZZARI (*de Liazariis*),[18] who had just taken his doctorate at Bologna (1319). Of these Frederick and Ricovero both left Opinions (*Consilia*), and Paul, among other works, a *Lectura* on the Clementines.

Cino himself, at the beginning of his time at Siena, delivered a famous Disputation on whether a citizen offending abroad could be punished at home.[19] He also gave numerous Opinions; was continually annotating his own Commentary on the Code (these notes form part of the text as later reproduced); and got as far as the second Book of the Digest in a *Lectura* intended to extend to all fifty Books.

Siena was in financial difficulties in 1326. Frederick stayed on, but Paul Lazzari and Ricovero accompanied Cino to Perugia, left orphan by James of Belvisio. Cino taught there for four years, then a year at Naples, perhaps a year at Florence, and another year at Perugia again (1332-1333) before retiring to his native Pistoia, to die at the turn of the year 1336 to 1337. He had lamented Dante's death in verse, and his own was lamented by Petrarch.

Of Cino's two companions at Siena and Perugia, Ricovero was teaching at Florence in 1334, but perhaps went back to Perugia. Paul Lazzari went back to Bologna in 1333, and stayed there till his death in 1356. Frederick Petrucci seems to have gone to Perugia in 1333,[20] the year in which Paul Lazzari left.

110. The Significance of Cino. — With Cino we seem to come out of a tunnel and into the broad light of day. The other Italian legists after Odofred left little trace, though they are continually cited at second and third hand as an exhibition of learning; but Cino is cited at first hand (to take an example at random) as late and as far as

---

16. 6 SAVIGNY 491 (a brief note); Fabio BARGAGLI, *Petrucci Federico da Siena, postglossatore canonista,* Atti del congresso internazionali di scienze storiche (Rome, 1904).
17. C.N.S. WOOLF, *Bartolus of Sassoferrato* (1913), at pages 404, 405.
18. R. CHABANNE, (1957) 6 Naz 1276. The date of his doctorate is from ALIDOSI, at page 190. Alidosi spells him "Leazari," but in modern Italian it is "Lazzari."
19. This Disputation is not lost (G.M. MONTI, note 12 above, at page 103), nor did it deal, except in passing, with the notorious summons by the Emperor Henry VII to King Robert of Naples to appear before him at Pisa. There is at least one manuscript, *Vat. Lat. 2656, from folio 112v, col. i; and Bartolo reproduces its substance in his commentary on the Conflict of Laws translated in (1970) 14 American Journal of Legal History, at pages 261 to 266. MONTI himself later found and edited this Disputation, but I have not been able to see his edition.
20. He was certainly there in 1341 and 1343. See ERMINI, *Perugia* (1971), at page 162.

Lyndwood's *Provinciale* in England (1422-1430). The change was the influence of the school of Orléans, which has indeed been detected in Italy before Cino, despite the disparaging remarks that occur so frequently. Martin Sylliman had echoed James of Révigny (without acknowledgment) as early as 1285,[21] and Dino did the same; and we have seen that Dino had the taste for cleverness which distinguished the French schools generally. Besides the dialectic approach, Cino took over the critical attitude towards the standard gloss; but he always treated it with respect, which after all was usually its due.

Cino had heard Peter of Belleperche once, when he delivered his visiting lecture at Bologna in 1300;[22] and he swallowed his writings hook, line and sinker — and with acknowledgment. He also, at least sometimes,[23] names James of Révigny where Peter had alluded to him without his name. It has been estimated that three-quarters of Cino's commentary on the Code is a reproduction of Peter of Belleperche,[24] although he does to some extent achieve the objective declared in his preface of reducing bulk by cutting out irrelevancies. There are 900,000 words in Cino, as against James of Révigny's million; and Cino also incorporated much from James of Arena and from his own master Dino, not to mention an unacknowledged theft from Nicolas Rufulo of Naples. His later annotations show that he had read the lectures of another Frenchman, William of Cunh[25] (paragraph 101 above), delivered after Cino's original text had been published.

111. The Commentary. — It was Cino's example that established the Commentary as the principle vehicle for juristic expression. Unlike the Orléans tradition, but like Odofred, Cino's work is written by himself in the first person: like both it is wholly innocent of systematic arrangement, simply following the order of the passages in the Code which provoked comment. Its literary ancestor then, far from being the Summa, was the Apparatus, from which it differs in two ways only: the substantial comments are much more so, while the purely verbal explan-

---

21. MEIJERS, *Orléans,* at page 118.
22. There is a persistent belief that Cino spent some early years in France, even at the feet of Peter of Belleperche: MEIJERS, *Orléans,* at page 116, dismisses this as a legend. It is impossible to go into this controversy, beyond saying that it is not so simple as that. And it is of no great importance, because Cino's dependance on Peter can all be traced to the latter's writings.
23. Several times on the first law of the Code, on the conflict of laws.
24. MEIJERS, *Orléans,* at page 120.
25. So Bartolo explicitly (on the conflict of laws), referring to an unacknowledged borrowing: translated at (1970) 14 American Journal of Legal History, at page 250.

ations almost disappear. New though this was to the "legist," the canonists had been writing Commentaries of this type since Innocent invented it a century earlier. It was a true perception of this ancestry that led to several of the canonist Commentaries being called "Apparatus," as indeed was Innocent's.

112. Padua: Richard and Olrad. — Meanwhile the school of Padua had been carried on by two students of James of Arena, RICHARD MALOMBRA (*Rizardus de Malumbris*)[26] of Cremona, and OLDRAD of LODI (*de Laude*, sometimes also *de Ponte*).[27] Richard (son of a less notable professor of both laws at Padua) had obtained his doctorate by 1289, presumably at Padua, and was teaching there by 1295 alongside of Nicolas Matarelli (paragraph 84 above). Oldrad had studied under Dino at Bologna as well as under James, and was himself "assessor" at Bologna in 1302-1303: by 1307 he was teaching at Padua.

Both left collections of Problems (*Questiones*), and Oldrad over 300 Opinions (*consilia*) which were long remembered. The writings of both on the Corpus Juris were in the nature of isolated Studies (*repetitiones*): it is a mistake to talk of "lectures" or "commentaries."

113. Richard of Malombra. — Richard is famous for his uncompromising condemnation of French-style cleverness in words worthy of John Bassian:[28]

> When deciding on whether a man is to be beheaded, distinctions between substance and accidents, or other syllogistic debate, are not the safest foundation; nor is this the method followed by our predecessors and ancient teachers ... They argued from the texts of our law nearest to the point in question. —

one might say by analogy rather than by deduction.

The succession to Naples at the death of Charles II in 1309 provoked a Disputation at Padua in which Nicolas Matarelli supported the son of his predeceased elder son, and Richard the second surviving son, Robert: Richard's view prevailed de facto. But this was the end of his time at Padua. The German Emperor Henry VII of Luxem-

---

26. 6 SAVIGNY 49; BESTA, *Riccardo* (1894).
27. 6 SAVIGNY 55; E. WILL, *Die Gutachten des Oldradus de Ponte* (Berlin & Leipzig, 1917).
28. The quotation (from Aubrey of Rosciate, paragraph 117 below) is printed by BESTA, *loc. cit.*, at page 175, and again by MEIJERS, *Orléans*, pages 110 and 111, note 394.

burg arrived in Italy in 1310 (paragraph 108 above), and Richard's imperialist views led to his leaving Padua in 1311. He had given advice to the Venetian government on occasion before, and was in its exclusive service as consultant from at least 1315 to his death in 1334. His stay in Bologna in 1328 was with leave of absence, in order to free himself from ecclesiastical censures: the "college of doctors" earned a rebuke for interceding for him. He did not teach there (he was getting on for 70), but he took part there in a public Disputation with James Buttrigar, James of Belvisio and Rainer of Forlì (paragraph 116 below).

114. Oldrad of Lodi. — Oldrad too left Padua after 1310. It is said that he went to Siena, to be expelled at the instigation of his fellow-teacher James of Belvisio, and then shortly to Montpellier before settling at Avignon; but the truth may be that he went straight from Padua to Avignon. There he taught at the *Curia Romana,* the papal university which had accompanied the papacy to Avignon, and was also consistorial advocate. He was still alive in 1337.

115. John Calderini. — James of Belvisio, Cino, James Buttrigar and John Andrews at Bologna, Richard and Oldrad at Padua, were all of the same generation. Paul Lazzari was half a generation younger, as was JOHN CALDERINI[29] who received his doctorate at Bologna in 1322. Though a layman, he taught canon law there alongside Paul Lazzari till his death in 1365. He was the adopted son of John Andrews, but his master is unknown. His principal writings were Opinions (*consilia*) which were much cited.

116. Rainer of Forli. — A more important name is RAINER of FORLÌ (*de Forlivio, Forliviensis*).[30] Of a prominent imperialist family, it is said that he spent his youth in exile from Forlì, at Ravenna; but he learnt his law at Bologna under Bertoluccio Preti,[31] and taught there from 1319 or so. He paid no attention to the secession in 1321, and in 1324 was salaried at 100 lire to lecture on the New Digest and (presumably from the beginning) on the Infortiatum, on which latter he composed annotations at Bologna. The Code and the Old Digest remained the preserve of James Buttrigar. Yet another civil convulsion

---

29. 6 SAVIGNY 109; J. RAFFALLI, (1937) 2 Naz 1191. The date of his doctorate is from ALIDOSI, at page 101.
30. 6 SAVIGNY 185; B. BRANDI, *Vita e dottrine di Raniero di Forlì* (Torino, 1885).
31. So he says himself, cited by BRANDI, *op. cit.*, at page 5. MEIJERS, *Orléans,* at page 119, makes him a student of Dino, but this is chronologically improbable.

led to the imposition of an interdict on Bologna in 1338, and after a short hesitation Rainer went with his students to Pisa, there to teach the Old Digest. Six years later (1344) the remarkable salary of 600 florins lured him to Padua, still teaching the Old Digest on which he published annotations (*additiones*, not a *lectura*) in 1355. He died at Padua in 1358. Besides his annotations Rainer left nineteen Studies (*repetitiones*) and five Opinions, and is also remembered for his annotations to William of Cunh and to Cino.

117. Aubrey of Rosciate. — Contemporary with Rainer, but not a teacher, was AUBREY of ROSCIATE (*Albericus de Rosate*),[32] under Bergamo. He was in practice at the bar in Rome and at Bergamo, and revised the statutes of the latter town about 1330. In 1336 he was sent to Avignon to obtain the lifting of ecclesiastical censures on Milan and Bergamo, and stayed there six years. In retirement he compiled a Dictionary of Civil and Canon Law founded on that of James of Revigny, and published it after 1350, since he refers to his presence in Rome for the Jubilee of that year: he died in 1354.

His more important work consisted of four Books of Problems on Local Legislation (*Questiones Statutorum*), and an enormous commentary on the whole of the Corpus Juris which often incorporates word for word not only his predecessors (including William of Cunh) but also his own Problems — but his Problems also refer back to his Commentaries, at least in the form in which they have come down to us. It was by his Problems that he was remembered: his Commentaries could not hold a candle to Bartolo (paragraph 121 below).

118. Signorolo. — To come back to Bologna (where James Buttrigar and John Andrews continued to teach till 1348, Paul Lazzari till 1356 and John Calderini till 1365) Rainer's chair there had been taken in 1338 by his student (and James Buttrigar's) SIGNOROLO OMODEI (*de Homodeis*)[33] of Milan, "unfit, but appointed for lack of suitable candidates" according to Rainer.[34] He took part in public Disputations at Pavia, Padua and Milan (but without teaching there), and retained his membership of the "college" of jurisconsults of Milan from 1330 to 1362. In 1351 he helped to revise the statutes of Milan. He died

32. 6 SAVIGNY 126; A. SALVIONI, *Intorno ad Alberico da Rosciate* (Bergamo, 1842).
33. A brief note in 6 SAVIGNY 497; A. LATTES, *Due giureconsulti Milanesi* (Milano, 1899, Rendiconti del Regio Istituto Lombardo), at pages 1017 to 1045.
34. Cited by BRANDI, *op. cit.*, at page 14. And see C.N.S. WOOLF, *Bartolus of Sassoferrato* (note 17 above), at page 399.

in 1371, leaving some Studies[35] and many Opinions: he relied much on Peter of Belleperche and more on William of Cunh. Signorolo was distinguished mainly by his vanity — he was an imperial count by his death — but was also given to noticing differences between civil and canon law.

119. Richard Salicet. — Another student of James Buttrigar[36] was the enigmatic RICHARD of SALICETO.[37] Saliceto is near Reggio, but the family, while keeping the local name, had been Bolognese and prominent in Bolognese politics for several generations. Richard was author of a Disputation at Bologna in 1331 or 1332, and continued to teach and to indulge in politics till 1353. To go over the chronological limits of this chapter, he was probably teaching at Padua from that date till 1362, and then at Florence from 1362. Bologna forfeited his property for this absence; but a turn of the political wheel brought him back in 1366, and he was sufficiently eminent to survive the next upheaval (in 1377) and die in peace at the beginning of 1379.

He left[38] Commentaries on the Code and on the Old Digest, and some Opinions and Problems have survived, mostly collected with other men's work. He did not give many Opinions, and did not waste much time on those he gave: his interest was mainly in the logical explanation and presentation of rules of law.

120. Other Universities. — The other towns of central Italy which had seen their opportunity in Bologna's difficulty did not last long as law-schools, with one exception. Arezzo's revival was momentary,[39] Siena's brief.[40] Pisa[41] did not survive the Black Death of 1348. Florence, which had tried for a few years from 1321,[42] tried again in 1348[43] in the hope of taking Pisa's place, but high rents kept students away.

---

35. Besides being confused with a later jurist of the same name, Signorolo has had his Study on the "law" *Cæsar* attributed to Bartolo, so that Rainer was long thought to have directed against Bartolo the invective provoked by it; and conversely Bartolo's Study on the "law" *cunctos populos* was sometimes attributed to Signorolo with a charge of plagiarising Bartolo. All this is disentangled by LATTES, *op. cit.*
36. MEIJERS, *Orléans,* at page 117.
37. BELLOMO, *Una famiglia* (1969).
38. BELLOMO, *Per un profilo* (1971). The commentaries disappeared, but Bellomo found fragments of them at Madrid: *loc. cit.,* at page 251.
39. 2 RASHDALL 8.
40. 2 RASHDALL 33.
41. 2 RASHDALL 45.
42. Torquato CUTURI, *Baldo degli Ubaldi in Firenze,* (1901) *L'opera di Baldo,* 365-385, at page 365.
43. 2 RASHDALL 48, 49.

The "one exception" was Perugia,[44] where James of Belvisio had taught from 1308 to 1321 and Cino from 1326 to 1333; and the reason for the exception was that BARTOLO of SASSO-FERRATO[45] taught there from 1343.

121. Bartolo. — For Bartolo (short for Bartholomew) was perhaps the most acute jurist of any age: he was the culmination of the renaissance of legal thought which began with Irnerius. He began to read law at the age of 13 or 14 under Cino at Perugia; and going on to Bologna, where his masters were James Buttrigar and Rainer of Forlì, took his doctorate there in 1334 at the age of 20. The next five years of his life are blank, except that at some time he held judicial office at Todi and at Pisa; but for us they are a very precious blank. Having drunk at both springs, from Cino the tradition of critical enquiry that went back to James Baldwin, and behind him to the Gosians, and from James Buttrigar and Rainer the painstaking solidity that, through Accursius, descended from the *nostri doctores,* he was occupied (as he says) in "studying and reviewing the books all by myself:" in Bartolo the two tendencies found their reconciliation. He taught law at Pisa for four years (1339 to 1343), during which time one of his colleagues was his old master Rainer,[46] and then at Perugia for fourteen years. He was only 43 when he died in 1357; but in this short life, besides many treatises and a few Opinions (*consilia*), he worked up from his lecture notes[47] the monumental Commentary on the whole of the Corpus Juris which fills nine folio volumes in the Renaissance editions. This bulk is due not to loquacity but to the range covered: the first nine books of the Code found only three-quarters of a million words of comment. Small wonder that he occasionally forgot to acknowledge a predecessor who had said the same thing: certain it is that he usually acknowledged scrupulously.

Plagiarism was nevertheless a charge brought early against Bartolo, and by those who admired him. No one thought till the sixteenth century of accusing him of bad Latin. Law-latin is indeed not Ciceronian — nor was the Latin of the Corpus Juris — and he whose acquaintance with Latin is only classical may well find it distasteful. Matters have been made worse by the ignorant "improvement" which his ma-

---

44. 2 RASHDALL 42.
45. WOOLF, *Bartolo* (note 17 above), pages 1 to 4.
46. *Op. cit.,* at page 398.
47. This is the conclusion drawn, after a painstaking analysis of annotations bearing Bartolo's name in the margins of the standard gloss, by Bruno PARADISI, *Le glosse di Bartolo da Sassoferrato,* (1971) ii La Critica del Testo, 575 to 618.

nuscripts suffered at the hands of Renaissance editors: Bartolo's pre-eminence excited more attention from them than they gave to most other medieval lawyers. Even so, it is quite unfair to call his Latin "uncouth."[48]

122. Bartolo's Influence. — To succeeding generations, until the strutting arrogance of the new learning found amusement in regarding as cobwebs all the patient labours of the Middle Ages, the authority of Bartolo was scarcely less than that of the Corpus Juris itself. Not everyone agreed with all he said, but he could be called their spiritual domicile in the sense that it was from him that they set out on their journey, and to him at the end of the day that they returned. He expressed thoroughly and completely, with a touch as light as it was sure,[49] the law as it had come to be lived but in the terminology and according to the concepts which Justinian had caused to be written down. One can only regret that, by choosing as his vehicle the Commentary, which followed strictly Justinian's somewhat haphazard arrangement, he deprived himself of the opportunity of constructing a whole whose coherence might have been evident rather than merely implicit. In this — perhaps in nothing else — France of the seventeenth and eighteenth centuries was superior to him.

48. As does WOOLF, *op. cit.,* at page 9.
49. The reader who desires to see for himself may turn to the translation of his Study on the conflict of laws in (1970) 14 American Journal of Legal History, 157 to 183 and 247 to 273.

Chapter VIII

Decline

(1350 - 1450)

Consilia

123. Perugia: Baldo and Angelo. — At the end of Bartolo's life two brothers, students of his, were teaching beside him: these were Baldo[1] and Angelo[2] Ubaldi, the elder more eminent, the younger more faithful to Perugia.[3]

Baldo, made doctor in 1344[4] by Bartolo, was doctor also of canon law, having studied under Frederick Petrucci. He taught first at Bologna, but came back to Perugia in 1351.

Angelo was made doctor in 1351, and remained teaching at Perugia, save for ten years in political exile (from 1384 to 1394 at Padua, perhaps Ferrara, Florence and Bologna) till 1399: he died at Florence in 1400 or soon after.

Baldo left Perugia in the year of Bartolo's death (1357), and stayed away (at Pisa and at Florence) for seven years; but between 1364 and 1390 he was absent only for a spell of three years, at Padua from 1376 to 1379. He was much involved in public life as well as in teaching, and he acquired an enormous reputation for wisdom. The last ten years of his life, from 1390 to 1400, he spent at Pavia in great

---

1. Scalvanti, *Baldo* (1901), pages 181-278; 6 Savigny 208-248.
2. Scalvanti, *Baldo* (1901), pages 279-298; 6 Savigny 249-255.
3. There was a third brother, Peter, who left no remarkable writing but taught canon law at Florence from 1362 to 1364 (paragraph 133 below), and at Perugia from 1364 to his death in 1412: Scalvanti, *Baldo*, pages 301-312. Many members of this family taught later without distinction.
4. He was not 17: he seems to have been born about 1319 — 6 Savigny 512 (app.): Scalvanti, *op. cit.*, page 190.

honour; but it is not true that he had a hand in the reform of that city's "statutes."[5]

As a commentator Baldo was more ponderous than brilliant; but his range was very wide, taking in civil law, canon law and feudal law, in which last he appears at his best. He commented at length on those Titles of the Corpus Juris (except the Authenticum) to which teaching had become restricted, and left also a *lectura* on the first three Books of the Extravagantes; annotations to the *Speculum Juris*; and notes (1391) on the *Libri Feudorum* and on the text of the Peace of Constance which became their Standard Gloss, as well as annotations to Martin Sylliman's work on feudal law. Besides commenting he left a very large number of those Opinions (*consilia*) which were sought from him on all occasions, and some Studies (*repetitiones*) of which at least one[6] dates from his stay at Florence. Five or six columns of notes on former law teachers are also attributed to him; but no copy is known to have survived.[7]

Angelo commented like his brother on all parts of the civil corpus (except this time the Institutes), and like him left Opinions.

124. The Succession at Perugia. — Far less distinguished was ANGELO PERIGLI[8] said to have been the grandson of Angelo Ubaldi, who may have been lecturing as early as 1399. He certainly lectured at Perugia from 1427 (with a gap of five years at Padua) till his death in 1447.

Alongside him the equally undistinguished JOHN PETRUCCI of Montesperello[9] taught from about 1420, and probably remained at Perugia till his death in 1464.

Angelo Perigli left a few Studies and Treatises, and John Petrucci some Opinions. The masters of both are unknown.

125. Bologna Civilians: Salicet. — Apart from the lustre which the personal pre-eminence of Bartolo and Baldo lent to Perugia, turbulent

5. Pasquale DEL GIUDICE, at pages 139 to 142 of *L'Opera di Baldo* (1901).
6. On the first "law" of the Code, *cunctos populos*: Torquato CUTURI, *Baldo degli Ubaldi in Firenze*, pages 365 to 385 of *L'Opera di Baldo* (1901), at page 377. The *repetitio* was edited by MEIJERS in 1939.
7. DIPLOVATATIUS cites it as the *Tractatus Famosissimorum Doctorum* — see comment by BESTA, *Baldo* (1901).
8. 6 SAVIGNY 480 (app.); DIPLOVATATIUS, page 368 (reading the date of his death as 1466, on which see 6 SAVIGNY 325, note b); ERMINI, *Perugia* (1971), vol. I, pages 505, 506.
9. 6 SAVIGNY 490 (app.); DIPLOVAVATIUS, page 370.

Bologna was still the only law-school where there were always teachers of repute, most of whom stayed there more or less permanently. Overlapping Richard Salicet (who died in 1379, paragraph 119 above) FRANCIS RAMPONI[10] (*de Ramponis, de Ramponibus*) taught civil law there for fifty years,[11] taking his doctorate in 1350 and dying in 1401: he left Opinions.

His contemporary, but less continuously at Bologna, was the last of the great civilian commentators, BARTHOLOMEW of SALICETO.[12] Salicet was in the direct line of Bologna tradition, having learnt his law (and inherited a bent for politics) from his uncle Richard Salicet, himself a student of James Buttrigar; and he taught at Bologna for most of his life, from 1363 to 1409, when illness caused his retirement. He died at the end of 1411.[13] His career at Bologna was broken by periods of exile (but still teaching) at Padua from 1370 to 1374, at Ferrara from 1389 to 1398, and at Padua again from 1400 to 1402. During his absence at Ferrara Angelo Ubaldi was teaching intermittently at Bologna (1388 to 1394).[14]

Salicet's great work, like Cino's, was on the Code: he began it during one stay at Padua and completed it a quarter of a century later on his next stay there in 1400. He also wrote a Commentary on the second half of the Old Digest, and left Opinions. Tradition did not prevent him from proposing and elaborating original solutions, and his arguments are persuasive.

126. Bologna Canonists: John of Legnano. — Bologna was also the principal home of the canonists, though they were no longer of the calibre of former generations. The Milanese JOHN of LEGNANO,[15]

---

10. 6 SAVIGNY 493 (app.); DIPLOVATATIUS, page 318.
11. With intervals of unspecified date and duration at Pisa, Ferrara and Padua; According to ALIDOSI, page 77, he was banished in December 1393 and restored only in 1399; but his name appears every year at Bologna from 1378 to 1401 in the *Liber Secretus*.
12. LIOTTA, *Bartolomeo da Saliceto* (1964).
13. The *Liber Secretus*, Vol. I, page 203, says December 1412, but it is the December before March (and July) 1412.
14. The *Liber Recordationum* of Gozzadino di Simonino Gozzadini, edited by Vittorio VALENTINI, (1969-70) 38 Studi Urbinati di Storia, Filosofia e Letteratura, pages 3 to 82, notes at page 33 that "Angelus de Perusia" began to lecture on the Infortiatum at Bologna in January 1391, but went back to Florence in February; and at page 35 that he began the New Digest in October 1391, the beginning of the academic year. The *Liber Secretus* does not mention him.
15. T.E. HOLLAND, *Joannis de Lignano, de Bello, de Represaliis et de Duello* (1917), pages x to xxvii of the Introduction, giving the date of his birth as about 1320; S. STELLING-MICHAUD, (1957) 6 Naz 111.

whose canon-law master was Paul Lazzari, was promoted doctor of both laws at Bologna in 1350 and 1351, and taught there till his death in 1383. In 1377 he had brought the city back to papal allegiance, and from then on was papal vicar as well as archdeacon.

Besides commenting on the whole corpus of canon law except the Sext, he wrote several treatises on war which have earned him the reputation of the precursor of public international law.

127. Peter of Ancarano. — Half a generation younger was the more celebrated PETER of ANCARANO,[16] near Orvieto. Besides studying under Baldo, he learnt both laws at Bologna, from John Calderini as an old man and from the youthful Salicet, taking his doctorate in 1370.[17] He seems not to have taught immediately, being occupied first as judge and deputy (*vicarius*) of the Podestà of Bologna. From 1384 to 1387 he was consultant to the Republic of Venice, and from 1387 to 1390 he taught at Siena. From 1390, and for most of the rest of his life,[18] he taught at Bologna, dying there in 1416.

His writings, which were much prized by his successors, included a Commentary on the Extravagantes and *lecture* on the Sext and the Clementines, together with numerous Studies (*repetitiones*) and Opinions, the latter not confined to canon law.

128. Antony of Budrio, John of Imola. — Two more canonists who were to be famous later qualified at Bologna at the end of the century: these were ANTONY of BUDRIO (*de Butrio*),[19] near Bologna; and another JOHN, this one Nicoletti of IMOLA.[20] They were born respectively about 1360[21] and 1370.[22] Both had studied under the civilian Francis Ramponi and the canonist Peter of Ancarano, Antony also under

16. BESTA, *Pietro da Ancarano* (1935), saying that he was born in 1333; Ch. LEFEBVRE and R. CHABANNE, (1957) 6 Naz 1464. ALIDOSI, at page 191, reveals the origin of the story that he was a Farnese: it is a funeral monument dated 1483 (cf. Encicl. It., vol. 14, page 828).
17. ALIDOSI, *op. cit.*, recording also his civic functions. LEFEBVRE and CHABANNE, *loc. cit.*, apparently in ignorance of this authority and finding no record of his activities before 1384, place his study under Salicet after 1376; but this is to forget that John Calderini died in 1365.
18. He taught from 1402 to 1405 at Ferrara, paragraph 129 below.
19. BESTA, *Antonio da Butrio* (1929); A. AMANIEU, (1935) 1 Naz 630; L. PROSDOCIMI, (1961) 3 D.B.I. 541. Cf. DIPLOVATATIUS, page 319.
20. D. STAFFA, *de Ioannis ab Imola vita et operibus,* (1937) 10 Apollinaris 76.
21. The date usually given — 1335 — is a guess backwards from the date of his death. 1360 is a more likely guess in view of the dates of his doctorates.
22. Between 1367 and 1372.

Salicet,[23] and John also under John of Legnano and under Antony himself. Antony took his two doctorates in 1384 and 1387,[24] John his civil-law doctorate in 1397.

129. Crisis at Bologna. — This is perhaps the point to interject that besides the doctors whose writings were thought worth preserving many others taught. We have mentioned only two civilians and two canonists teaching at Bologna in 1381, but there were 23 salaried professors there in that year, their salaries ranging from 100 to 620 lire.[25] The regular complement of civilians was a dozen, teaching not more than 250 students:[26] the whole student body can therefore not have been greater than 500 by this date.

By 1400 turbulence had gone too far: in the din of ejectment and counter-ejectment the professors' salaries were not regularly paid. Not all of them reacted, but Salicet departed from Padua at this time. When he came back in 1402, Peter of Ancarano, Antony of Budrio (returned in 1399 from six years' teaching in Florence) and John of Imola accepted an invitation to FERRARA[27] for three years. Peter and Antony taught canon law there, John civil law.

Next year Balthasar Cossa, said to have been doctor in both laws from Bologna and certainly archdeacon there from 1392 to 1396, cardinal in 1402, recaptured the city for the papacy and established a firm government. Peter and Antony went back in 1405, and Antony died there in 1408: besides Opinions he left a voluminous Commentary on the Extravagantes, and commented also on the Sext.

John too left Ferrara in 1405, but went to Padua and taught canon law there till 1410. Order having returned to Bologna, he came back to teach canon law there till 1415, then civil law (the New Digest and the Infortiatum). 1416 is the date of his lament that doctors and students were deserting Bologna, and indeed the student body was

---

23. John perhaps also from Baldo: so SAVIGNY on Baldo, note 1 above.
24. Where (and whether) he taught before 1390 is not clear; but he taught for a year at Perugia (1390-91) and two years at Bologna (1391-93) before going to Florence for six years.
25. 1 RASHDALL 211.
26. In the eight years from 1378 to 1386 (the doctorate took eight years) 129 doctors graduated: *Liber Secretus,* Vol. I, pages 1 to 40. Making allowance for two incomplete years 1382-83 and 1383-84) and the inevitable drop-outs, 250 is the highest possible number for students at any one time.
27. Ferrara was not at this time a regular law-school, but Angelo Ubaldi seems to have taught there in 1386, as did Salicet from 1389 to 1398: it had received university status in 1391, but was closed three years later — LIOTTA, *Bartolomeo da Saliceto,* at page 514.

little more than half what it had been thirty years earlier.[28] From 1420 John was teaching canon law again, and continued to do so (with an interval of two years, 1430-1432, at Padua) until his death in 1436. Unlike some of his brethren he had not been too good a salesman of himself; but he was a first-rate scholar, with a library of 600 books — for whose loss in a fire in 1432 he was compensated from public funds — and is credited with an imposing number of students who afterwards acquired fame.[29] Besides Opinions he left Commentaries on the first three Books of the Extravagantes and on the Clementines, and also on the Infortiatum and on the New Digest. These are distinguished more by the completeness of his citation of earlier authorities than by his own contribution; but his mastery of both laws led him often to interpret each by analogy from the other.

130. Dominic of San Gimignano. — Not much younger than John of Imola was DOMINIC of SAN GIMIGNANO[30] (*de Sancto Geminiano*) near Florence, whose master was Antony of Budrio. He too taught at Bologna and died there before 1436. Besides the usual Opinions, he commented on Gratian's Decreta as well as on the Extravagantes and the Sext, and left also *summule* on the Extravagantes and a *lectura* on the Sext which has some merit.

131. John of Anagni. — Finally in this series a third JOHN, of ANAGNI[31] (*Ananias*), is said to have been a student of Peter of Ancarano (as well as of Florian of St Peter, paragraph 132 below), but did not take his degree of doctor of both laws till 1423, seven years after Peter's death when he was himself already in middle age.[32] He taught at Bologna for twenty years more, before exchanging his lectern for practice at the bar in 1443: he died in 1457, leaving Commentaries on the Extravagantes and the Sext, as well as Opinions. One of his students had been the Venetian Pietro Barbo, later Pope as Paul II (1464 to 1471).

---

28. Between 1410 and 1418 79 civilian doctorates were conferred — *Liber Secretus*, pages 193 to 232 of Vol. I.
29. STAFFA, *loc. cit.*, lists Angelo of Arezzo and Angelo de Gambilonibus as if they were separate persons; but his careful footnotes reveal that he has taken the first name from Panciroli and the second from Mazzetti. Panciroli gives him also Alexander, aged 13 at John's death (paragraph 148 below), and Staffa throws in Jason, aged 1 at John's death (paragraph 160 below). R. NAZ, (1957) 6 Naz 109, copies Staffa's list, but without the footnotes.
30. R. NAZ, (1949) 4 Naz 1410.
31. J. VIRET, (1957) 6 Naz 88.
32. He was 70 when he made his will in 1446: he was therefore born about 1376.

132. Bologna: the Succession. — The teacher who provided continuity in the generation[33] after Salicet was FLORIAN of Castel SAN PIETRO,[34] (*de Sancto Petro*), made doctor of civil law by Salicet in 1385 and also doctor of canon law. After a spell at Siena he taught at Bologna from 1397[35] to 1430, and again from 1438 till his death in 1441. He left comments on some passages of the Code and the Old Digest.

The New Digest and the Infortiatum were taught from 1415 to 1420 by the canonist John of Imola (paragraph 129 above), and from 1424 to 1429 by Paul of Castro (paragraph 134 below).[36]

Overlapping him was ANGELO Gambiloni of AREZZO (*Aretinus*),[37] who had learnt his law from Paul of Castro (at Siena or at Florence?), John of Imola (at Bologna) and Florian: it was Florian who presented him publicly as doctor in 1422, four years after his "private"

---

33. Some minor teachers at this time perhaps deserve footnote mention. MACAGNAN AZZOGUIDI, doctor in 1370, left a volume of Opinions which had a certain vogue: ALIDOSI, page 168 (his father's name was Gregory, and he is to be distinguished from another doctor of the same name two generations earlier (1309), son of Dr Bliobarigio Azzoguidi. Alidosi identifies the earlier doctor with him who, according to Caccialupi died aged 25, but without date. See DIPLOVATATIUS, page 287).

    Bartholomew Salicet's son JAMES of SALICETO was made doctor in 1380 and died six years after his father in 1418: *Liber Secretus,* vol. I, pages 6 and 233; DIPLOVATATIUS, page 323 *in fine;* 6 SAVIGNY 497 (app.).

    His second cousin, also JAMES of SALICETO (son of Robert), took his doctorate in 1395, but died in 1399 of the plague: *Liber Secretus,* pages 93, 94; BELLOMO, *Una famiglia,* page 407.

    The Venetian ZACHARIAS of TREVISO (*Trivisanus*) took his doctorate in 1396 (*Liber Secretus,* page 99), but is not known to have composed anything but a Disputation abridged by Peter of Ancarano (paragraph 127 above) commenting on c. *canonum.* Zacharias became Podestà of Florence, senator at Rome, and (in 1404) "Captain" of Crete for the Venetians. After the Venetian conquest of Padua in 1405 he became "captain" of that city, and died in 1414 — ZONTA, *Zabarella,* at page 41.

    MATTHEW MATHASILANI was made doctor in 1398 (*Liber Secretus,* page 122) and left a few treatises.

34. DIPLOVATATIUS, page 328; 6 SAVIGNY 487 (app.).
35. This is the date of his "aggregation" into the "college" of civilian doctors: *Liber Secretus,* vol. I, page 111.
36. He is not mentioned in the *Liber Secretus* between 1430 and 1438 (pages 99 and 167 of vol. II). ALIDOSI mentions an absence at Ferrara (page 78), but says that he came back to Bologna in 1432: the date is evidently wrong, but the place may be right. His death is in the *Liber Secretus,* vol. II, at page 180.
37. DIPLOVATATIUS, page 374, making him also a student of the two Raphaels (paragraph 135, 139 below): if this is right Angelo must have studied at Padua. 6 SAVIGNY 480 (app.) is very sketchy. Cf. E. ALBERTARIO, (1932) 16 E.I. 357, citing (for the printing of his criminal work) KANTOROWICZ, *Gandinustext* (1922), pages 30 and following.

examination. Angelo wrote on the last Book of the Institutes, *de Actionibus* (1443), and also on criminal law (*de Maleficiis*). He was still in Bologna in 1445, but went to Ferrara in 1450[38] and died there in 1451. His treatise on criminal law was printed as early as 1472 (together with the work of Albert Gandini on the same subject), and his *de Actionibus* in 1473.

ANTONY Mincucci of PRATOVECCHIO[39] is also said to have studied under Paul of Castro and Florian. He was teaching at Bologna as early as 1410, and taught also at Padua, Florence, and on more than one occasion at Siena; but he did not take his doctorates till later: 1424 in civil law and 1458 in canon law. He seems to have been more a canonist than a civilian, never appearing as member of the civilian's "college" and acting several times as deputy (*vicarius*) of the Archdeacon;[40] but his achievement was in the realm of feudal law. After he had recast the two *Libri Feudorum* in six Books, his students at Padua (where he was teaching in 1428 and 1429) suggested to him that he should do the same for James Dove's gloss, and he published this while teaching at Florence in 1431. The whole was consolidated and revised in 1442, a quarter of a century before his death in 1468.

133. Florence: Lapo (and Baldo). — The other law-schools had for the most part to be content with short visits from the illustrious — which does not mean that teaching was discontinuous. FLORENCE exceptionally had the canonist John LAPO of CASTIGLIONCHIO (*Castileoneus*)[41] for a quarter of a century, from 1353 to 1379. He had studied at Bologna under John Calderini and John of Legnano. His principal work was a collection of specimen pleadings, in the sense of written arguments (*Allegationes Juris*).

Lapo taught without salary at first — not without income, for he would charge fees from his students in the old way. It was only in 1357[42] that the city government made provision for teachers. Baldo

---

38. According to Diplovatatius he was invited there by Borso of Este, who succeeded only in 1450.
39. 6 SAVIGNY 294-311; but the surname "Mincucci" is never attributed to him by the *Liber Secretus*, nor currently by contemporaries. BESTA, *Mincuccio Antonio*, (1934) says he was born about 1380. See also P.S. LEICHT, *Antonio da Pratovecchio nelle sue relazioni con Padova e con Venezia*, (1922) 7 Studi e Memorie per la Storia dell' Università di Bologna, at pages 15 and following.
40. In 1436 (before his canon-law doctorate), 1441, 1442, 1450 — *Liber Secretus*, pages 145, 189, 195, 256.
41. J. VIRET, (1957) 6 Naz 110.
42. Torquato CUTURI (note 6 above) at page 365.

began to teach there (after two years at Pisa) in 1358, and in 1359 was given Florentine citizenship.[43] He was joined by his brother PETER UBALDI for canon law in 1362;[44] but Peter went back to Perugia in 1364, followed by Baldo in 1366. From 1362 to 1366 Richard Salicet was teaching at Florence: his salary was 800 gold florins as against Baldo's 300. Lapo began to be paid in 1367; but in 1378 the law-school was closed,[45] and in 1379 Lapo was exiled for political reasons. On the re-opening of the school in 1385 the canonist Zabarella[46] (paragraph 138 below) took his two doctorates there and lectured on the Sext and the Clementines for five years till 1390: during this period Angelo Ubaldi taught civil law in 1388.[47] Antony of Budrio taught canon law for six years from 1393 to 1399, in which year Angelo came back, but in retirement.[48]

It was in 1406 that Florence conquered Pisa and carried off as spoils of war the ancient manuscript of the Digest which has since then been called the *Littera Florentina.* The talisman was surrounded with such superstitious awe that few were allowed even to see it, none to read it.

134. Paul of Castro. — Florence provided longer anchorage than any other Italian city for PAUL of CASTRO[49] (west of Lake Bolsena in Roman Tuscany). He was studying under Baldo at Perugia in 1375, though barely 15 years old, and later under Christopher Castiglioni (paragraph 135 below) apparently at Siena. Paul himself seems to have taught at Siena before taking his doctorate in both laws at Avignon in 1385: the reason for his going to Avignon is not known; but he stayed there till 1402, being *auditor* for part of this period for Peter Corsini, the "Florentine" Cardinal; and we have a collection of 137 Opinions given there.

Coming back to Italy he was at Florence till 1424 (except for a long interval at Siena from 1404 to 1411),[50] teaching certainly some of the time, probably all of it: his teaching spread the knowledge of

43. *Loc. cit.,* at page 366.
44. *Loc. cit.,* at page 374.
45. ZONTA (1915), at page 6.
46. *Op. cit.,* pages 6 and following.
47. SCALVANTI, *Baldo* (1901), at page 289.
48. *Loc. cit.,* at page 296.
49. 6 SAVIGNY 281-293; Niccolo DEL RE, *Paolo di Castro,* (1970) 82 Studi Senesi 194.
50. He was podestà at Viterbo for six months in 1404. Assertions of teaching at Perugia are due to misunderstanding of one Opinion concerning a case at Perugia.

John Faure's works which he had acquired at Avignon.[51] In 1415 he took part in the reform of the Florentine "statutes."

Paul then taught at Bologna from 1424 to 1429 (the New Digest and the Infortiatum), and at Padua from 1429 to his death in 1441. His *lecture* on all three Digests and on Books 1 to 4 and 6 and 7 of the Code have the quality of great clarity.

135. Pavia. — PAVIA in the Duchy of Milan was fostered as a matter of political prestige by the ambitious Gian-Galeazzo Visconti, and received its constitution as a university by a bull of the Roman Pontiff Boniface IX in 1389. Next year the celebrated Baldo accepted a chair there, and continued to teach at Pavia till his death there in 1400.

Before Baldo his student JOHN-PETER FERRERS[52] (*Joannes Petrus de Ferrariis*) of Parma, had been appointed there, and in 1400 began a collection of precedents of "libels" (statements of claim), called *Practica Judicialis*.

CHRISTOPHER of CASTIGLIONE (*Castellioneus*)[53] of Milan, who was probably also appointed at this time, was another student of Baldo's. He must have taught elsewhere before — he was already over 40[54] — but the order in which he taught in various places is not clear. Though he left only a few Opinions his adventurous mind[55] was influential in his teaching: he made a name for himself by disrespect for the "received view" (*communis opinio*).

The "two Raphaels" as they are always called were both students of this Christopher: they were RAPHAEL FULGOSIO[56] of Piacenza, student also of Salicet, who was appointed at Pavia in the same year, 1389; and RAPHAEL of COMO[57] (*Cumanus* or *Comensis*), also appointed there and probably at the same time. The Opinions of these two were collected together; and Raphael Fulgosio is known to have written on the Code and on the Old and New Digests.

In 1399 Raphael Fulgosio took the law-school with him to his home-town of Piacenza. Christopher of Castiglione probably went there at the same time, since he is said to have taught at Piacenza (without date). From there the two Raphaels went on to Padua,

51. MEIJERS, *Orléans*, at page 114.
52. DIPLOVATATIUS, page 326; 6 SAVIGNY 486 (app.).
53. DIPLOVATATIUS, page 315; 6 SAVIGNY 484 (app.).
54. He was born in 1345 according to ERMINI, *Castiglione* (1931).
55. So DIPLOVATATIUS; cf. 6 SAVIGNY 273, note 1, citing Jason.
56. DIPLOVATATIUS, page 339; 6 SAVIGNY 270-276, giving his date of birth as 1367.
57. DIPLOVATATIUS, page 340; 6 SAVIGNY 486 (app.).

Fulgosio certainly in 1407, and both died there in 1427 of the plague. Christopher went back to Pavia, and was still there at his death in 1425.

136. Parma. — The law-school at Parma was re-opened in 1412 with the appointment of the canonist Nicolas Todeschi (paragraph 141 below), who stayed there for six years before going on to Siena. Raphael Fulgosio was there in 1413; and at some unspecified time Christopher of Castiglione was also teaching at Parma.

137. Padua. — Padua, of earlier and of later fame, was host to Richard Salicet for a period up to 1362; to his more celebrated nephew Bartholomew Salicet from 1370 to 1374; to the canonist Lapo in exile from Florence from 1379 to his death in 1381; and to Baldo's brother Angelo from 1384 to 1386.

138. Zabarella. — Padua's own son, FRANCIS ZABARELLA,[58] came home in 1390. He had begun his legal studies at Padua, but transferred to Bologna (with many others) when Padua was at war with Venice. At Bologna he studied under Salicet[59] and John of Legnano;[60] but it was at Florence that he obtained his two doctorates in 1385. He then taught canon law at Florence till 1390. Returned to Padua to lecture on the Extravagantes, he continued to teach there till 1411, undisturbed by the Venetian conquest of Padua in 1405: the Venetians not only preserved the law-school but subsidised it. He left Commentaries on the Extravagantes and on the Clementines; but politics (paragraphs 145, 146 below) monopolised his attention from 1411 to his death in 1417.

139. Padua, the Succession. — Meanwhile Bologna's troubles sent Salicet back to Padua in 1400 till 1402, and John of Imola from 1405 to 1410. Padua kept the two Raphaels for twenty years or so, from 1407 till their deaths in 1427, with an interval at Parma: Fulgosio lectured in the mornings on the Code and the Old Digest, and he of Como in the evening on the Infortiatum and New Digest. Antony of Prato Vecchio was teaching there in 1428 and 1429; Paul of Castro from 1429 till his death in 1441; John of Imola (again) from 1430 to 1432; and Angelo Perigli perhaps from 1431 to 1436. Probably beside

58. ZONTA (1915), fixing his birth in 1360 instead of the earlier guess of 1335.
59. So SAVIGNY on Salicet. On Baldo, SAVIGNY makes Baldo also Zabarella's master — and Baldo was teaching at Padua from 1376 to 1379. ZONTA names only John of Legnano.
60. He was *licentiatus* at Bologna in 1383.

them taught another Paduan, JAMES ALVAROTTO,[61] a student of Zabarella who commented on the *Libri Feudorum,* and died there in 1453.

140. Siena. — To come back to Tuscany, Siena had no well-known professor till 1375. It would appear that Christopher of Castiglione was teaching here at this time, and that it was here that Paul of Castro learnt from him. Certain it is that Paul himself was teaching here before his doctorate at Avignon, perhaps from 1380. Florian of St Peter taught here at the beginning of his career, from 1385 to perhaps 1397. For three years from 1387 to 1390 Peter of Ancarano was teaching canon law here.

141. The Panormitan. — A canonist of high repute who stayed at Siena for twelve years (1418 to 1430, after a year at Bologna and six at Parma) was the Sicilian NICOLAS TODESCHI[62] (*de Tudeschis*: his father was German), born at Catana in 1386. He learnt his law at Padua from Zabarella,[63] and left a very influential Commentary on the Extravagantes, begun in 1422. He ceased to work on it in 1437, in which year he also finished a collection of leading points in canon law (*Thesaurus singularium in jure canonico decisivorum*). He also delivered himself of Studies and Opinions. Meanwhile his diplomatic intrigues had led the Pope to attempt to placate him (in 1425) with the abbacy of Santa Maria de Maniaco at Messina; and the King of Sicily to attract him (in 1434, after he had ceased to teach)[64] with the Archbishopric of Palermo: he owes to these appointments his more usual appellations of the SICILIAN ABBOT (*Abbas Siculus*) and the PANORMITAN, meaning "of Palermo." He died of the plague in 1445.[65]

142. Ludovic of Rome. — Siena was also the scene of the brief teaching career of a canonist of great promise, LUDOVIC Pontano of Spoleto, called of ROME (*de Roma, Romanus*).[66] He studied at Perugia and (under John of Imola) at Bologna, taking his doctorate in 1429. He

61. DIPLOVATATIUS, page 366; 6 SAVIGNY 479 (app.), dating his birth to 1385.
62. BESTA, *Niccolo de' Tedeschi* (1934); Ch. LEFEBVRE, (1957) 6 Naz 1195.
63. He is also conjectured to have studied at Bologna: LEFEBVRE and CHABANNE on Peter of Ancarano (note 16 above) suggest Peter as his master there; but the same LEFEBVRE, on the Panormitan himself, suggests Antony of Budrio.
64. He had another year, 1431-32 at Bologna, before devoting himself wholly to politics.
65. Besta says 1466, but this must be a mistake.
66. DIPLOVATATIUS, page 352; 6 SAVIGNY 489 (app.); R. NAZ, (1957) 6 Naz 684. The *Liber Secretus* describes him as Lodovicus de Roma at his private civilian examination in 1427, and as Ludovicus Pontanus de Roma at his public doctorate in 1429 — vol. II, pages 70 and 95.

soon exchanged teaching for practice, first at Florence, then at Rome; and he left principally Opinions, but also treatises and a collection of leading points (*singularia*). He was killed by charcoal fumes when sleeping in a tightly closed room in 1439, at the age of 30.

143. The Great Schism.[67] — These three generations lived through the anguish of the Great Schism and its aftermath. Pope Gregory XI, said to have studied law under Baldo, brought the papacy back to Rome from Avignon in 1377; and his death a little over a year later precipitated a double election. One Pope stayed in Rome, the other went back to Avignon. After thirty years of wrangling the tide set in favour of an imposed solution — and of a Council as the instrument of this imposition.

The conciliar solution is ususally attributed to the theological faculty of Paris, as opposed to the canon lawyers of Bologna, but there was no such opposition. It is true that the first reaction of the lawyers in 1378 was to ask which election was valid; but when it became clear that those in control of physical force were not interested in validity, the lawyers were not behind the theologians in the search for arguments to justify conciliar supremacy.

144. Legal Opinions. — At the beginning of the schism in 1378 John of Legnano sent a strong letter of remonstrance to the French cardinals before they elected the first Avignon Pope of this line. This did not prevent the election; and equally without influence on the Avignon party was Baldo's Opinion, after the election but still in 1378 (when he was at Padua), in favour of the Roman Pope. These first salvoes were followed in 1380 by further Opinions from both Baldo (at Rome) and John of Legnano in the same sense. Salicet also gave an Opinion in this direction; but the Neapolitan jurists were for the Ultramontanes.[68] Ten years later there was a shift: the Roman Pope called Zabarella from Florence in 1390 for consultation on means to bring the scandal to an end, and his advice (which was not well received) was joint abdication.

Baldo[69] came slowly round to a universal council, though only too well aware of the difficulty that a council had no juridical existence

---

67. In this and in the next four paragraphs the information on each individual comes from the same sources as have been already cited: footnotes are added only for matter both new and not of general knowledge.
68. LIOTTA, *Bartolomeo da Saliceto* (1964), at page 513.
69. For the development of his thought see James A. WAHL, *Baldus de Ubaldis: a Study in Reluctant Conciliarism,* (1974) 18 Manuscripta 21-29.

unless summoned by a pope — and the right pope. Baldo died in 1400; and in 1405 Peter of Ancarano at Bologna published the first of a series of seven Opinions, this one in reply to his former student Innocent VII of Rome. By the end of the series, in 1409, he had arrived at the conclusion that if the two Popes could not settle their differences their Cardinals had the legal power and duty to call a Council and impose a solution.

Antony of Budrio had been the Roman Pope's ambassador to his Avignon rival, and had procured an agreement in 1407 which was not implemented: with his last breath (1408) he held it to be the Cardinals' duty to summon a Council.

In 1409 Zabarella published a treatise on the schism: of the eight solutions which he suggested the first was a Council called by the Cardinals. Opinion thus came into line, just in time, with the facts.

145. Pisa. — The Council which met in 1409 at Pisa had been summoned there by the Cardinals of both obediences in defiance of their two masters. The aged Peter of Ancarano was in attendance as representative of the University of Bologna, as were two young Bologna lawyers, Dominic of San Gimignano (as vicar-general to the Bishop of Modena) and Antony of Prato Vecchio, at that time in practice at Bologna.

This Council purported to depose both popes and to elect a third; and on his death they elected Cardinal Balthasar Cossa, papal governor of Bologna since 1403: he took the name of John XXIII. The other two popes not recognising their deposition, John had some difficulty in maintaining himself; but in 1411 Zabarella gave up his chair at Padua to join him: John made him Bishop of Florence and Cardinal.

146. Constance. — Still finding no way out of the impasse, John found himself forced in 1413 to summon another Council at Constance, sending Zabarella to preside and Peter of Ancarano and Raphael Fulgosio as his personal representatives. The Council's first significant act was John's deposition in 1415. The Roman Pope then summoned the Council afresh (thereby legitimating it in the eyes of his more logical supporters), abdicated and died. The Avignon Pope found himself deserted; and the practical question then arose of how to elect a new one.

Zabarella had continued faithful to John XXIII until the latter's behaviour made this impossible. He was now able, on behalf of the

Cardinals, to turn aside the current of thought in favour of election by the whole Council and to procure agreement on an electoral college composed of the Cardinals and (for this one election) of an equal number of other members of the Council. He died in 1417, a month before the election by this body of Martin V, who was soon universally recognised. Peter of Ancarano had died a year earlier, on his return from Constance to Bologna.

The Council was dissolved, but not before it had provided for regular periodical synods, of which the first met at Siena (1423 to 1424) and the next at Basel in 1431.

147. Basel. — The epilogue also involved the lawyers. Nicolas Todeschi intrigued against Pope Martin V at the synod of Siena while he was professor there; but (after receiving his Sicilian abbacy) he seems to have worked loyally to execute Eugenius IV's mandate in 1432 to persuade the officially dissolved synod at Basel to disperse. In this he was unsuccessful, and then tried to work out a compromise. The Pope not playing, Nicolas reverted to conciliar supremacy, encouraged by the gift of the Archbishopric of Palermo from Eugenius' enemy the King of Sicily. Antony of Pratovecchio was also at Basel, arguing for conciliar supremacy and the power of the Emperor to summon a council: Venice charged him in 1435 with obtaining the lifting of the excommunication imposed by the Council on the Republic.

In 1436 Nicolas was back at Basel in the King's interest, together with young Ludovic of Rome who died on this mission in 1439. In that year the synod elected another conciliar Pope, who took the name of Felix V: at Felix' hands Nicolas received the crowning dignity of the Cardinalate. He died in 1445, before Pope and King made up their quarrel (in 1449) and Felix and the Council accordingly collapsed.

CHAPTER IX

Mediocrity

(1450 - 1550)

MORE CONSILIA, FRENCH CUSTOMS

148. Alexander of Imola. — Bologna was to have one more generation of eminence. While Antony of Pratovecchio continued to teach there till 1468, civil law was concurrently taught by Alexander of Imola till 1477, and canon law by Andrew of Sicily till 1478.

ALEXANDER Tartagni[1] of IMOLA[2] studied[3] at Bologna under Angelo of Arezzo and John of Anagni,[4] and took his doctorates there, in civil law in 1445,[5] and in canon law perhaps in 1447 or 1448.[6] In 1446 he was assessor to the *Conservator Justitiae* at Bologna, and then in practice at Imola till Bessarion's "reform" of the law-school in 1450. From then on (with two intervals, at Ferrara from 1457-58 to 1460-61 and at Padua from 1467-68 to 1469-70)[7] he taught civil law at Bologna

---

1. A. SABATTANI, *de vita et operibus Alexandri Tartagni de Imola,* a doctoral thesis written before the war but first published in (1971) 83 Studi Senesi 171-273 = (1972) 27 Quaderni di Studi Senesi.
2. The Latin is *Tartagnus* or *de Tartagnis*: the form Tartagna was adopted later by the same family. In any case it was little used in contemporary references.
3. He was a student in civil law in 1438, being then "*adultus,*" meaning between 15 and 21. There is thus no need to doubt his age at death as inscribed on his tomb, according to which he was born in 1423 or 1424: *loc. cit.* at pages 15, 17, 21. ALIDOSI's date of 1438 must refer to this document (page 12).
4. Not John of Imola: the Opinion describing him as "my master" is not Alexander's, though printed with Alexander's Opinions. In any case John of Imola died in 1436. Not impossible but still improbable as a master is Paul of Castro who was still alive in 1438, but at Padua. In truth both of them were masters of Alexander's master Angelo of Arezzo (paragraph 132 above).
5. SABATTANI, *loc. cit.,* at pages 22-24 (*Liber Secretus,* vol. II, page 228).
6. He describes himself as *doctor utriusque juris.* There is no record of his canon-law doctorate, but for the years 1447 and 1448 the records at Bologna are missing.
7. He did not teach at Padua in 1446, or at Reggio in 1447 and 1448, or at Pavia in 1449 and 1450, or at Padua again in 1457-58: *loc. cit.,* pages 25-27, 35.

till his death in 1477. At Bologna he lectured always in the evenings on the New Digest and the Infortiatum, reserving the day for his practice at the bar — a very lucrative practice, for his Opinions were eagerly sought from all over Italy, and were highly paid for. In his youth he was in straitened circumstances, but he died extremely wealthy.

For all that, he never allowed his practice to interfere with his teaching, the record of which is to be found in his *lecture* on selected Titles of the New Digest and Infortiatum, together with his annotations to Bartolo whose commentaries were also compulsory lecture-material. His *lectura* on three Books of the Code and on some authentics records his teaching at Ferrara,[8] as does probably that on the Old Digest.

But the work which deserved his future fame was seven large volumes of Opinions, of which the first four were selected by Alexander himself and printed just after his death. A fifth was in print in 1490, and the last two perhaps not until 1521. These Opinions are both lucid (if somewhat prolix) and convincing.

149. Andrew of Sicily. — ANDREW BARBAZZA of Messina in SICILY (*Andreas Barbatias, Andreas Siculus*)[9] had studied medicine at Bologna before turning to the law and taking his canon-law doctorate there in 1439: in 1441 he was still only "licentiate" in civil law.[10] His canon-law master was John of Imola. After a spell at Ferrara he taught at Bologna from 1442 till a year before his death in 1479. He was a man of great pugnacity, in very lucrative practice at the bar, and Opinions were sought from him by many governments and rulers: King John II of Aragon made him his official adviser at the end of 1466.[11] Besides these Opinions, printed as early as 1489, he left various Studies on the Extravagantes and a Commentary on the first three Books of that compilation (and on the Clementines), and he annotated the Panormitan's commentary.

150. Ludovic Bolognini. — LUDOVIC BOLOGNINI (*de Bologninis*)[12] studied under both Alexander of Imola and Andrew of Sicily, and

8. It is dated to 1460. He did not write on Book III of the Extravagantes or on the Sext or on the Clementines: *loc. cit.*, pages 85 to 88.
9. A. AMANIEU, (1935) 1 Naz 520; LIOTTA, *Barbazza* (1964).
10. *Liber Secretus*, page 194: "... loco archidiaconi Andreas de Cicilia decretorum doctor et in jure civili licentiatus ..."
11. ALIDOSI, page 11.
12. DIPLOVATATIUS, page 420; 6 SAVIGNY 356-371; L. FRATI, *Lodovico Bolognini*, (1908) I.ii Studi e memorie per la storia dell' università di Bologna 117-142, supplemented by Luigi SIGHINOLFI, *Angelo Poliziano, Lodovico Bolognini, e le Pandette Fiorentini*, (1921) 6 *ibid.*, 189-308, particularly pages 239 to 255 and 259 to 292.

took his two doctorates in 1469 and 1470. He taught civil law at Bologna from 1469 to 1473, from 1489 to 1495, and from 1506 to his death two years later: 18 years in all. In the intervals he was six years teaching at Ferrara from 1473 to 1479; three years at Rome as consistorial advocate from 1486 to 1489; eleven years from 1495 to 1506 with no apparent salaried occupation and mainly at Florence. One reason for this last absence was political: he had welcomed the invasion of Italy in 1495 by Charles VIII of France, and had dedicated to him a book printed in that year; but Charles was soon rolled back, and Bologna captured by a dictatorship. When Pope Julius II recovered Bologna in 1506 Ludovic returned. Next year he was Gonfaloniere della Giustizia and also sent on an embassy to France: he died at Florence in 1508 on his way home.

During this time, besides giving Opinions on his own account, he annotated those of John of Anagni, as well as Matthew Mathasilani's treatise on Succession, and also made an index to Alexander's Opinions; but it is as a textual critic that he is best known. An early humanist, he was already dissatisfied with the received text of the Corpus Juris when he took his doctorate, and attributed much of the dreary controversy surrounding it to textual corruptions. An essay, probably in this sense, was suppressed in 1485 as insulting to his more conventional colleagues, an episode which no doubt explains his departure for Rome in the following year. His Roman appointment took him often to Florence, and Lorenzo the Magnificent procured for him the unprecedented privilege of not only seeing but reading the jealously guarded Littera Florentina. Back in Bologna, his lectures immediately reflected the variant readings he had found, and he was continually sending for more from his humanist friend Angelo Poliziano who was interested in the Pandects from a literary point of view. The work which Ludovic dedicated to Charles VIII was called *Novae Interpretationes*, and was largely founded on these variants. His later prolonged stay in Florence was occupied with making a complete list, for the printing of which Julius II issued a privilege in 1506; but his death appears to have prevented printing till the 1516 edition at Lyon. He also prepared an edition of the Novels in the original Greek, with a new Latin translation to supersede the Authenticum, which was the basis of Haloander's edition of 1531.

In addition to its own doctors Bologna was host to John Campeggi (paragraph 157 below) from 1488 to 1490, and again from 1505 to 1511; and to Bartholomew Sozzini (paragraph 154 below) from 1494 to 1507, except for an absence from 1498 to 1501 at Padua.

151. Perugia. — Angelo Perigli and John Petrucci were teaching at Perugia till their deaths in 1447 and 1464 respectively.

Half a generation younger BENEDICT Benedetti (*de Benedictis*) CAPRA,[13] who had "heard" John of Imola, taught canon law from 1442 till his death in 1470:[14] his nickname means "she-goat" and referred to the timbre of his voice. He was twice prevented, in 1452 and 1458, from transferring to Ferrara, and in the latter year John and he recast the Perugian municipal "statutes." Besides his *lectura* on the Extravagantes, which he was writing continously from 1442 to 1459, and various Studies on the Clementines, he finished in 1458 a collection of "Conclusions" on matters coming up frequently in court and explained to the unintelligent. His Opinions were collected and printed as early as 1476.

Apparently younger was another canonist, PHILIP FRANCHI (*Francus, de Franchis*)[15] who taught from 1458 to 1461, and again (after an interval at Pavia and Ferrara) from 1467 to his death in 1471. His principal work was a *Lectura* on the Sext, but he also annotated Zabarella on the Clementines, wrote on the Extravagantes and (so it is said) on the Old and New Digests, and collected Problems.

NICOLAS Ubaldi (grandson or great-grandson of Baldo's brother Peter), commonly called of PERUGIA (*Perusinus*),[16] taught both laws at Perugia till called to Rome in 1471 as *auditor sacri palatii.* He wrote on the first part of the Code, and also a treatise on Intestate Succession.

Among the students of Angelo, John Petrucci and Benedict Capra — all three in each case — were John-Baptist Caccialupi, who taught for a few years at Perugia before transferring to Siena in 1451 (paragraph 152 below), and PETER-PHILIP della CORGNA (*Corneus, de Cornea*).[17] The latter taught at Perugia from 1450 or so (with absences at Ferrara from 1469 to 1471 and at Pisa from 1473 to 1477) till his death in 1492. He left four volumes of Opinions, and also *lecture* on the Code and on the Old Digest. Perugia has no later names.

---

13. P. PALAZZINI, (1946) 19 Apollinaris 259.
14. Not 1465 and not 1480.
15. ERMINI, *Perugia* (1971), at page 547.
16. DIPLOVATATIUS, page 402.
17. DIPLOVATATIUS, page 407 (giving his age at death as 72, so that he would have been born about 1420); 6 SAVIGNY 485 (app.); ERMINI, *Perugia* (1971), page 510.

152. Siena. — MARIANO SOZZINI (*Socinus*),[18] to be distinguished from his grandson of the same name (paragraph 168 below), was a Sienese and friend of Aeneas Sylvius Piccolomini, later Pope as Pius II. A true child of the Renaissance, he was a man of many accomplishments; but juristic talent was not one of them. He had nevertheless sat at the feet of the Panormitan[19] in his native city, and he taught both civil and canon law there till his death in 1467. He left, besides Opinions, Commentaries on Books II, IV and V of the Extravagantes. He began the legal education of his son Bartholomew, who taught at Siena for two years (1471-73) before transferring to Pisa (paragraph 155 below).

Another teacher here was MARTIN Garazzi of LODI[20] (*de Garatis, Laudensis*), who began his career at Pavia, but from 1445 and for many years taught at Siena. He wrote on the *Libri Feudorum*.

Less undistinguished was JOHN-BAPTIST CACCIALUPI (*de Caccialupis*)[21] of San Severino in the March of Ancona. He had studied at Perugia under Angelo Perigli, John Petrucci and Benedict Capra[22] and had taught there for a few years before coming to Siena in 1451. Here he composed (in 1467) a treatise entitled How to Study (*de Modo Studendi*), but full of biographical details of his predecessors and much used by Diplovatatius (paragraph 161 below). It claims to be founded on Baldo's similar work, which Caccialupi may have found at Perugia. Over the next ten years he was composing Studies on the Code[23] and the Old Digest, and left also Opinions. He was called to Rome in 1484 as consistorial advocate and to teach canon law, and died there in 1496.

153. Francis of Arezzo. — FRANCIS Accolti of AREZZO (*de Accoltis, Aretinus*)[24] learnt his law at Siena from Antony of Pratovecchio and from Ludovic of Rome. It is dubious whether he taught first at Bologna; but by 1450 he had been teaching for some time at Ferrara. He transferred to Siena in 1451, the same year as John-Baptist Caccia-

---

18. 6 SAVIGNY 342-345 (dating his birth to 1401); R. NAZ, (1965) 7 Naz 1064.
19. STAFFA on John of Imola (paragraph 129 above) lists Mariano among John's students, citing Mariano on Extravagantes V.i.17.
20. DIPLOVATATIUS, page 367 (spelling his name *de Caraziis*); R. NAZ, (1957) 6 Naz 837.
21. Giuliana D'AMELIO, (1972) 15 D.B.I. 790 (dating his birth to about 1420).
22. So he says, as quoted by DIPLOVATATIUS on Benedict, at page 383.
23. That on the "law" *cunctos populos* is dated by D'AMELIO, *loc. cit.*, to between 1472 and 1477.
24. Anon., (1960) 1 D.B.I. 104. He was a little over 50 in 1468, which fixes his birth about 1415.

lupi, and stayed there for six years. After four years at Ferrara again (1457-1461) and five years in the diplomatic service of Francesco Sforza, he came back to Siena in 1466 and stayed there till 1479. He then went to Pisa till 1484, after which he retired to Siena and died there in 1489.

He was more noted in the realms of philology, philosophy, music and poetry than in law: his law-latin, infiltrated by Italian as law-French was by English, seemed so barbarous beside his poems and works on other subjects that some doubted whether they could come from the same pen. He left a few Opinions and also *lecture* (perhaps really Studies) on most parts of the Digest and on Book II of the Extravagantes.

Philip Decio (paragraph 155 below) came to Siena in 1484 when Francis left, and stayed there for three years, and again for a spell up to his death in 1536.

154. Pisa. — The law school at Florence continued to languish, and in 1472 it was decided to transfer it (but not the manuscript of the Digest) to the older university at PISA. No pains were spared to make the new foundation a success, and the foremost names in the mediocre band available were engaged to teach there. Peter-Philip della Corgna came from Perugia in 1473 (and stayed for four years); BARTHOLOMEW SOZZINI (*Socinus*)[25] in the same year from Siena. Bartholomew had learnt his law there from his father Mariano (and perhaps from Caccialupi),[26] and, after a spell at Bologna under Alexander of Imola and Andrew of Sicily, from Francis of Arezzo. He taught at Siena for two years, and then for twenty-one at Pisa (1473 to 1494) before passing on to Bologna where he died in 1507. He had a great reputation as a teacher, and left Opinions and Studies on the Infortiatum.

A year again after Bartholomew another student of Francis of Arezzo[27] transferred to Pisa from Ferrara. FELINO SANDEO[28] owed his first name to having been accidentally born at Felina under Reggio; but he belonged to Ferrara (paragraph 156 below). He stayed thirteen years at Pisa (1474 to 1487)[29] before being called to Rome by Pope Innocent VIII: Pope Alexander VI (Roderick Borgia) made him

25. 6 SAVIGNY 345.
26. So DIPLOVATATIUS, at page 398, and 6 SAVIGNY, at page 324, both on Caccialupi.
27. So DIPLOVATATIUS, at page 414, and 6 SAVIGNY 328, on Francis of Arezzo.
28. DIPLOVATATIUS. at page 414; E. ALBERTARIO, (1936) 30 Encicl. It., 632; R. NAZ, (1953) 5 Naz 827.
29. Innocent was Pope from 1484 to 1488: the precise date of Felino's departure comes from the biography of Philip Decio (paragraph 156 below).

bishop of Penna in 1495. Translated to Lucca in 1449, he died in 1503. He was survived by Opinions and "Collections" and a commentary on the fifth Book of the Extravagantes, besides a history of the Kings of Sicily and Naples from 537 to his own day, printed in his lifetime.

Francis of Arezzo himself joined his two students at Pisa in 1479, and stayed there till 1485. He taught Charles Rovini here, and Rovini began his own teaching career at Pisa: for its continuation see paragraph 161 below.

155. Philip Decio. — Meanwhile from Pavia (paragraph 159 below) came the canonist George Natta, who stayed at Pisa till at least 1478, and also Lancelot Decio of Milan for ten years, from 1473 to 1483.

Lancelot was apparently accompanied by his younger brother PHILIP DECIO,[30] still a student (Jason had been his master at Pavia). Philip received his doctorate at Pisa from his brother's hands in 1476, and began to teach the Institutes there. But he soon set the new academic community by the ears with his gift for making his opponent in debate appear ridiculous. Particularly resentful were Bartholomew Sozzini and Felino, who refused to appear against him; and after Lancelot had gone back to Pavia Philip had to withdraw to Siena in 1484. Felino's move to Rome allowed Philip back in 1487, and in Felino's canon-law chair. His old master Jason paid a year's visit to Pisa in 1488-89. Philip co-existed peacefully with Bartholomew during the latter's seven remaining years, and both were masters at this time of John Medici, son of Lorenzo the Magnificent, and later to be Pope as Leo X.

When Bartholomew went in 1494, Philip was the only remarkable teacher left at Pisa, and he went too in 1501, first at Padua and then in 1505 to Pavia (for his adventures there and further north, see paragraph 159 below). He was back at Pisa in 1515, and in 1517 he settled a curriculum still in force there in Savigny's time. He later transferred again to Siena, where he was still alive in 1536, over eighty years old.

He left Commentaries on feudal law and on "actions" (both printed at Pavia while he was still at Pisa, in 1483); on the Code and all three Digests (printed at Milan, 1507 to 1513); and on the Extravagantes; and also a treatise on Maxims (*de Regulis*).[31] But it was his Opinions that attracted some attention from posterity.

---

30. 6 SAVIGNY 374; cf. R. NAZ, (1949) 4 Naz 1059.
31. Peter STEIN, *Regulæ Juris* (1966), page 162.

156. Ferrara. — Ferrara continued to attract occasional teachers, among them Andrew of Sicily from 1439 to 1442. In 1442 this school formally recovered university status, and soon after Francis of Arezzo made his first stay there (1448), together with his compatriot Angelo of Arezzo who died there in 1451. Francis came back in 1457 to teach together with Alexander of Imola: both left in 1461. Philip Franchi taught there for some years up to 1467; and he died there in 1471. From 1469 to 1471 Peter-Philip della Corgna taught there, and Ludovic Bolognini from 1473 to 1479. Felino, a child of Ferrara, studied there under Francis of Arezzo (before 1461)[32] and Philip Franchi, and was himself teaching canon law there from 1466 to 1474 before going on to Pisa. Considerably later Charles Rovini taught there for some time.

157. Padua. — Padua had no celebrated teacher for forty years after the death of the two Raphaels in 1427; and after that had, as before, only short visits from such teachers. Alexander of Imola was there from 1467 to 1470; Jason from 1485 to 1488; Bartholomew Sozzini from 1498 to 1501; Philip Decio from 1501 to 1505; and Charles Rovini up to perhaps 1510.

More permanent was the Bolognese JOHN-ZACHARIAH CAMPEGGI (*Campesius*)[33] who had learnt his law from Alexander of Imola at Bologna and Francis of Arezzo at Pisa. He had taught at Bologna before obtaining his doctorate in 1473, and then taught at Pavia for ten years. From 1483 to 1505 (except for two years at Bologna, 1488 to 1490) he taught at Padua, then went back to Bologna but died in exile at Mantua in 1511. He left a treatise on Dowry (*de Dotibus*) printed at Pavia in 1477.

A Paduan doctor who did not teach was JOHN Bertachini of FERMO (*Firmianus*),[34] near Ancona. After a short judicial career he was called about 1480 to Rome as a consistorial advocate, and there composed a legal Encyclopedia (*Repertorium Juris*) in alphabetical order of subject matter. He died about the turn of the century.

---

32. Francis was out of teaching between 1461 and 1466 (paragraph 154 above); but if Felino was aged 60 when he died (as DIPLOVATATIUS says), then he was under 20 in 1461.
33. P. PASCHINI, (1930) 8 E.I. 597.
34. M. CARAVALE, (1967) 9 D.B.I. 441, giving his birthdate as about 1448. From this date it follows that his doctorate is likely to have been conferred after Alexander's departure in 1470 and before Jason's arrival in 1485. Also that 1480 is a likely time in the pontificate of Sixtus IV (1471-1484) for his summons to Rome.

158. Feudal Law.— Feudal law continued to attract attention, as we have seen from time to time. The impulse given to its study by Antony of Pratovecchio's re-ordering of the *Libri Feudorum* in 1442 was felt towards the end of the century at opposite ends of Italy. MATTHEW D'AFFLITTO (*de Afflictis*)[35] (1448 to 1528) was professor at the university of Naples before taking his seat on the bench, and wrote various works on Neapolitan feudal and constitutional law. Later in date of composition, but by an elder writer, were the twin Treatises on Feudal Law (*de Feudis,* in form a clause-by-clause commentary on a specimen feudal grant) and on Homage and Feudal Services (*de Homagiis et Roydis*) published in 1487 by GIACOMINO Micheloni of SAN GIORGIO (*Jacobinus de Sancto Georgio*).[36] This teacher had learnt his law at Turin, and taught there from at least 1452 to his death in 1494, as well as serving the Duke of Savoy diplomatically and judicially. Besides these treatises he left 50 Problems on feudal law; Opinions; and *lecture* on the Code and the Old Digest, which had been the subject of most of his teaching.

159. Pavia. — Pavia suffered a decline in the middle half of the fifteenth century: the only professor of slight note after the death of Christopher of Castiglione in 1425 was Martin of Lodi who taught there from 1483 to 1444. FRANCIS CORTI (*Curtius*)[37] the elder taught there continuously (but without distinction) from about 1450[38] to 1495. Canon law was taught by Philip Franchi for some years from 1461, and by GEORGE NATTA[39] of Asti from 1468 for a few years. He went on to Pisa, but in 1478 his sovereign the Marquess of Montferrat appointed him to his council. He died in 1495, leaving Studies and treatises. John Campeggi taught for ten years at Pavia before going on to Padua in 1483.

LANCELOT DECIO[40] of Milan studied under Alexander of Imola, evidently from the dates at Bologna, and began to teach at Pavia in

35. 6 SAVIGNY 479 (app.).
36. Gian Carlo BURAGGI, *Giacomino da San Giorgio* (1914, the second number of *I Giureconsulti dell' Università di Torino nel Quattrocento*), a copy of which I owe to the good offices of Professor Giuseppe Treves of Turin University. He calls Jason (paragraph 160 below) his "preceptor," but Jason began to teach when Giacomino was already *doctor utriusque juris.*
37. DIPLOVATATIUS, page 418; 6 SAVIGNY 486 (app.).
38. This is a pure guess, based on his not having taught elsewhere than at Pavia. His only solid date is 1485.
39. BESTA, *Natta, Giorgio* (1934).
40. 6 SAVIGNY 372. His father was a nobleman with another Arthurian name, Tristan.

1464. Apart from his ten years at Pisa from 1473 to 1483 he taught all his life at Pavia, dying in 1503: he left commentaries on the Code, the Old Digest and the Infortiatum.

Pavia had been under French occupation with the rest of the Duchy of Milan since 1499, and still was when Philip Decio arrived there in 1505, two years after his brother's death. There he upheld (almost alone) the supremacy of a Council over the Pope; but the Council in question (called by the Emperor Maximilian and Louis XII of France) was a fiasco, and Philip was declared schismatic in 1512. The sack of Pavia by Swiss troops in papal pay cost him his library of 500 volumes and all his manuscripts. The French being at the same time ejected from Milan, Louis XII made Philip judge (*conseiller*) in the Parlement at Grenoble, which did not prevent his appearing as professor at Valence and raising the number of law-students from 25 to 400. Three years later the French were back in Milan under Francis I, and Philip with them; but he preferred to go back to Pisa.

160. Jason. — After the deaths of Alexander of Imola and of Andrew of Sicily in 1477 and 1479 (paragraphs 148 and 149 above) the mantle of Bologna fell on Pavia; and the reason for this was the eminence of JASON del MAYNO.[41] Bastard son of a Milanese nobleman, he studied under Alexander at Bologna[42] and began to teach at Pavia in 1467: he taught there solidly, with the exception of four years, till his death in 1519. He was an excellent lecturer, and besides four volumes of Opinions left *lecture* on various passages in the Corpus Juris which show a competent grasp and synthesis of his predecessors' ideas; but when he is original he is not impressive. It is said of Jason that he was the last of the old school, as Alciati (paragraph 168 below), his student but 60 years his junior, was the first of the new.

161. The Last Generation in Italy. — Philip Decio, as we have seen, was still alive at a great age at Pisa in 1536.

At Pavia the younger FRANCIS (or ROCH) CORTI[43] (nephew of his elder namesake) taught alongside Jason, and died in 1533 leaving Opinions.

41. 6 SAVIGNY 397, giving his birth-date as 1435.
42. Not at Pavia, where Alexander never taught, nor in 1450-51 when Jason was only 15: SABATTANI (note 1 above), pages 89, 107.
43. 6 SAVIGNY 436 (app.); cf. BESTA in *Storia di Diritto Italiano* (ed. Pasquale DEL GIUDICE), Vol. I (*Fonti*, 1925), at page 896 — "Curzio Rocco," but in the index "Corti, Rocco = Curzio Rocco," dating his career 1470-1515.

CHARLES ROVINI (*Ruinus*)[44] of Reggio, born in 1456, studied under Francis of Arezzo[45] (evidently from the dates at Pisa — paragraph 154 above), and taught at Pisa, Ferrara, Pavia (where he was about 1500), Padua and finally Bologna from 1511[46] to his death in 1530. He left principally Opinions which when printed filled five volumes.[47]

Charles was succeeded briefly at Bologna by the Bolognese LUDOVIC GOZZADINI,[48] who died in 1536 leaving Opinions. He was teaching already at Bologna, as had been HIPPOLYTUS MARSILI (*de Marsiliis*).[49] Hippolytus took his degree in 1480, and having spent his youth in administration and at the bar, taught civil law at Bologna from 1497 till his death in 1529. He wrote on criminal procedure as well as collecting the Leading Points (*singularia*) for which he is best remembered.

ALBERT BRUNI,[50] (1467-1541) studied for seven years at Turin under the feudalist Jacobin of St George before passing to Pavia in 1496 to hear Jason, Charles Rovini and the elder Francis Corti: it was at Pavia that he received his doctorate in both laws. He then practised at the bar, and for the last twenty years of his life was Advocate Fiscal to the Duke of Savoy. He left Opinions on almost every point of feudal law, and also a digest (*repertorium*) of this branch of the law, besides treatises mainly on statute law.

THOMAS DIPLOVATATIUS[51] (1468-1541) was born on the island of Corfu, but early brought to Italy. He studied both civil and canon law at Bologna — and also between 1485 and 1488 at Padua, where Jason was his master — and took his civil-law doctorate, being already doctor of canon law,[52] at Ferrara in 1490. From 1494 he held public office at Pesaro, which despite absences elsewhere became his home town. He seems to have read nearly everything written by his pre-

---

44. ALIDOSI, page 59; 6 SAVIGNY 496 (app.).
45. 6 SAVIGNY 328 (on Francis of Arezzo).
46. Guido ZACCAGNINI, *Storia dello Studio di Bologna durante il Rinascimento* (1930), at page 198. ALIDOSI's date (at page 59) of 1514 must be that of his "aggregation" into the "college" of doctors. In 1515 he was given Bolognese citizenship. The date suggested for Pavia comes from the career of Alberto Bruni below.
47. Lyon 1557. Lincoln's Inn has, besides this, a Study on the Title *de Novi Operis Nunciatione*, printed at Bologna at the end of 1535.
48. ZACCAGNINI, *op. cit.*, at page 205. ALIDOSI says (at page 159) that he took his doctorate in 1486, but also that he was 57 at his death in 1536.
49. ALIDOSI, page 152; 6 SAVIGNY 489 (app.); ERMINI, *Marsili* (1934).
50. Piero CRAVERI, *Bruno, Alberto,* (1972) 14 D.B.I. 647.
51. ERMINI, *Diplovataccio* (1931).
52. Mario ASCHERI, *Saggi sul Diplovatazio,* (1970) 82 Studi Senesi 340, at page 344.

decessors; but his title to fame is his compilation of their lives and works, *de Claris Jurisconsultis* (1511). He also prepared editions of Bartolo and of Alexander of Imola.

162. France: Universities and Customs. — In France legal literature of note no longer issued from the universities. Attention was more and more reserved for the Customs, and literature consisted of commentaries on them written by practitioners — who had indeed been formed in romanising universities but who did not usually teach there. For universities continued to exist, and indeed new foundation with law faculties were made. Duke Philip the Good of Burgundy founded DÔLE in 1423,[53] and his cousin Duke John IV of Brabant (whose Duchy was soon to be united to Burgundy) founded LOUVAIN in 1426.[54] In 1432[55] King Charles VII founded POITIERS, his temporary capital while the English had Paris.

In the next generation King Louis XI founded VALENCE in Dauphiné in 1452[56] while still Dauphin, and BOURGES (where he was born) in 1464.[57] There were several German foundations earlier than this; but the only one relevant here is TÜBINGEN in the south-west, dating from 1477.[58]

The earlier group of foundations belongs chronologically to the last chapter, as does the first writer now to be mentioned.

163. Masuer, Gui Pape, Stephen Bertrand. — JOHN LE MASUYER (*Masuerius*),[59] born at Riom in Auvergne, studied at Orléans at the beginning of the fifteenth century before practice at the bar in the Sénéchaussée of the Bourbonnais: he died in 1450. His Court Practice (*Practica Forensis*) was in form a descendant of the *Ordo Judiciarius* so popular earlier; but like it dealt with substantive law. The substantive law on which it was founded was that of Auvergne and the Bourbonnais, but Masuer was a universalist as well as a Romanist, and his work was influential everywhere in France.

GUI PAPE[60] of Dauphiné, a generation later, studied at Montpellier and also at Pavia and Turin before returning to Grenoble. In 1444

53. 2 RASHDALL 191.
54. *Op. cit.*, at page 264.
55. *Op. cit.*, at page 194.
56. *Op. cit.*, at page 201.
57. *Op. cit.*, at page 205.
58. *Op. cit.*, at page 279.
59. J. BRISSAUD, *Cours d'Histoire générale du Droit français* (1904), at page 295.
60. G. LETONNELIER, (1953) 5 Naz 1009.

he was elevated to the bench of what was then the Council but later became the *Parlement* of Dauphiné. In 1461 he was dismissed, having incurred the displeasure of Louis XI, and returned to the bar: he died in 1477. While on the bench he made a collection of 632 *Quaestiones* purporting to be "Decisions of the Parlement of Dauphiné," though in fact only 130 of them rested on such decisions. He also left Opinions.

A generation later again, STEPHEN BERTRAND[61] read law for seven years at Valence and at Toulouse; but he attained no higher degree than that of bachelor before setting up in practice at Avignon. He was 35 when in 1469 or so he went to Carpentras, in the papal county of the Venaissin, and stayed there. He was papal judge there from 1476, and about 1490 at last took his doctorate. From 1497 he was President of the Apostolic Chamber (final Appeal), and from 1507 Vice-Regent of the County. He died at the turn of 1516-17, having collected close on 4000 of his Opinions in thirty volumes: they were later printed in eight volumes. He was well acquainted with earlier jurists, French and Italian, and — a new phenomenon — occasionally cites classical authors.

164. Nicolas Everard. — The flame then flickers further afield, in the Low Countries. NICOLAS EVERARD[62] (1462-1532, of Zeeland) studied at the University of Louvain. After his doctorate in 1493 he went to the bench, and was President of the Supreme Court (for the whole of the Spanish Netherlands) at Malines. He left Opinions, but his famous work, entitled *Topica seu de Locis Legalibus* (1516), was of the kind earlier called *Questiones*. His approach was distinguished by an interest in the philosophical basis of the law.

165. Bohier, Chasseneuz. — Meanwhile in France the reduction of the Customs to written form was well under way, and we have a group of three jurisconsults who commented on them. NICOLAS of BOHIER (Boerius, 1469-1539)[63] learnt his law at Pisa and Montpellier, and from 1497 was in practice at Bourges. He was also professor at the law-school there. In 1507 he was appointed to the bench of the *Parlement* of Bordeaux, where he died thirty years later. He left a Commentary on the Customs of Berry (1508, before their reduction to writing in 1539), and also a collection of the Decisions of the "Senate" of Bordeaux.

---

61. Paul OURLIAC, *Etienne Bertrand* (doctoral thesis, Paris, 1937).
62. 6 SAVIGNY 464.
63. M. PREVOST, (1954) 6 D.B.F. 782.

BARTHOLOMEW of CHASSENEUZ (*Chassenaeus*, c. 1480-1544)[64] of Autun in Burgundy studied at Dôle, Poitiers, Bologna, Turin (1497) and Pavia (1499), where Jason was his master.[65] He was promoted doctor of both laws in 1502, and after legal employment with the French forces of occupation (paragraph 159 above) returned to Autun in 1506. Practice at the bar left him time to compose his Commentaries on the Custom of the Duchy of Burgundy, reduced to writing in 1458 before reunion with the crown of France. This was first published in 1517, and revised in 1528 after his elevation to the bench. He sat in the *Parlement* of Burgundy from 1525 to 1531, and after a year at the *Parlement* of Paris was appointed President of the *Parlement* of Aix, where he died. He left also a collection of Opinions.

166. Tiraqueau, Imbert. — ANDREW TIRAQUEAU (*Tiraquellus*, 1488-1539)[66] learnt his law probably at Poitiers, and in 1512, at the age of 24, was appointed judge at Fontenay-le-Comte. This town, the capital of Lower Poitou, was then a focus of intellectual and legal culture: Rabelais learnt his law there and was Tiraqueau's close friend. Tiraqueau had at least roughed out by 1513 a Commentary on the whole of the Custom of Poitou, but this was never published: he did publish at that date an extract on Matrimonial Property (*de Legibus Connubialibus*), and in 1535 a commentary on the "law" in the Code dealing with the revocation of donations. His writings earned him an invitation to the *Parlement* of Bordeaux (which he refused) and in 1541 appointment by the intervention of King Francis I to that of Paris. Here he published two more extracts from his Commentary on the Custom of Poitou, in 1543 on the *Retrait Lignager* (pre-emption by the heirs-at-law) and in 1549 on Nobility and the Right of Primogeniture. At his death in 1559 he had another extract ready on Prescription, and this was published a year later. Before he died his work on Matrimonial Property had reached its fifth edition (1554). The principal characteristic of his work is its enormous erudition, exhibited by strings of references to previous writers.

A later judge at Fontenay-le-Comte was JOHN IMBERT,[67] who as a young advocate published in 1542 four volumes on French procedure, *Institutiones Forenses Galliae*, and in 1556 an *Enchiridion Juris Scripti*

64. Roman D'AMAT, (1959) 8 D.B.F. 714.
65. He says so in his Commentary.
66. Jacques BREJON, André Tiraqueau (doctoral thesis, Poitiers, 1937).
67. G. RENARD, (1886) 20 **Grande Encyclopédie 587.**

Galliae Moribus et Consuetudinibus Recepti (handbook of Roman law as received in French usage and custom).

167. Dumoulin. — A little younger than Chasseneuz and Tiraqueau was CHARLES DUMOULIN (*Molinaeus,* 1500-1566),[68] the last and greatest of this group. Son of a Parisian advocate, he himself joined the Paris bar after study at Paris, Poitiers and Orleans — we are not told which university gave him his doctorate. A difficulty of speech made him prefer consultation to pleading, and as early as 1525 he had given an Opinion which is the foundation of the modern French theory of community property in marriage. This was only one aspect of the Custom of Paris on which he was working all his life: his commentary on the Title regarding Fiefs (of the 1510 rescension of the Custom) appeared in 1539 and made him famous, besides being the source of many judgments of the *Parlement* of Paris. He was a passionate advocate of the unity of law, but not on the basis of Roman law which he insisted had no more than persuasive force in France: he desired the underlying unity of the multitudinous Customs to be brought out, and published a detailed plan of operation in his *Oratio de Concordia et Unione Consuetudinum Franciae.* Not that he neglected Roman Law. Besides editing (and annotating) the Opinions of Stephen Bertrand (1532) and of Alexander of Imola (1543), Dino's commentary on the maxims which formed the last Title of the Sext (1548),[69] and the maxims of Philip Decio (1553), he wrote his own treatises on loans on interest (1545), damages (1546), donations in marriage contracts and "inofficious" wills and gifts (1550).

He announced his conversion to Calvinism in 1542, but was not disturbed till the publication of virulent anti-papal invectives in 1552 made it necessary for him to withdraw from France. In 1553 he was appointed senior professor of law at Tübingen in south-west Germany, but his impossible behaviour[70] limited his stay there to a year. After a spell in prison at Montbéliard, he taught again for part of a year at Dôle and Besançon in Franche-Comté: Besançon was then no more than an annexe of Dôle. During these university years (which termin-

68. R. FILHOL, (1953) 5 Naz 42. We must be duly grateful for this biography, and for the editor's overlooking the somewhat shadowy connection between Dumoulin and canon law.
69. See Peter STEIN, *Regulæ Juris* (1966), at page 162: the outlook has changed little since Dino.
70. Jean CARBONNIER, *Dumoulin à Tubingue,* (1936) 60 Revue générale du Droit de la législation et de la jurisprudence, 194 to 209.

ated with his return to France in 1557) he composed a Commentary (more accurately a series of Studies) on the first six Books of the Code and on part of one Title of the Digest: these were published on his return.

Back in France he published his Commentary on the second Title (*des Censives*) of the Custom of Paris (1558), and a collection of his Opinions (1560). His conversion to Lutheranism in 1556, and his attacks on both Catholics and Calvinists, led to his being harassed by both sides in the Wars of Religion. He made no further progress on the Custom of Paris beyond brief sketches, but in 1566 he published a *Grand Coustumier* in two volumes, containing all the Customs with his own notes. He died at the end of this year.

Dumoulin's greatness lay in his ability to see what the law ought to be in the new social circumstances of his time; but he was a true Bartolist in his endeavours, sometimes specious, to show that that was in fact the law contained in the texts, romanist or customary. It was these arguments which smoothed the way for acceptance of his detailed ideas by the courts, by the revised Customs, by subsequent writers, and eventually by the Civil Code which finally accomplished the unification of which he dreamt. In his harsh Latin Dumoulin was also of the Middle Ages; but in his limitless vanity he belonged to the New Learning, to which we must now briefly turn.

Chapter X

Epilogue

(1520 - 1600)

New Learning

168. Alciati. — After classical studies at Milan Andrew Alciati[1] passed in about 1507 to Pavia, and there heard Jason and Philip Decio. Going on to Bologna about 1511 he had Charles Rovini as master; but he took his doctorate in both laws (in 1516) at Ferrara, where he had never studied. While he was at Bologna he published notes on the last Three Books of the Code (printed in 1515) and a restoration of the Greek passages in the Digest. These were reprinted at Milan in 1518 with six Books of *Paradoxa* which earned him great fame. Up to 1518 he had been in practice at the bar, but from that year till 1533 was his French period: four years' teaching at Avignon, and again (after five years back in Italy at the bar in Milan) from 1527 to 1529; and then four years at Bourges. His lectures on the Titles of the New Digest at Avignon and Bourges were printed as he went along. In 1533 the Duke of Milan recalled him to teach at Pavia, though with absences of four years each at Bologna (1537-1541) and at Ferrara (1542-1546). He died in 1550, having acquired a reputation for going wherever the highest salary was offered — which would not nowadays be considered very reprehensible, and was a characteristic of many eminent professors. Of more lasting importance was his ability to combine in his teaching a practitioner's realism (he left large numbers of Opinions) with a feeling for history and a classical Latin style. For the distinguishing mark of the new learning was its latinity, the balanced and rounded phrases of Cicero replacing the rough and direct language at which the men of the Renaissance turned up their fastidious noses. Rhetoric, which had been banished from the law by Irnerius, came back in this sixteenth century; but the content of what was taught did

1. R. Abbondanza, (1960) 2 D.B.I. 69.

not at first significantly change. It was not until 1540 or so that Bartolo was decisively dethroned.[2]

Contemporaneously with Alciati the younger MARIANO SOZZINI[3] (1482-1556), student of his uncle Bartholomew, taught at Siena, Pisa, Padua and (from 1543) Bologna: he left Opinions.

169. Anthony Agostini. — Canon law was classicised a generation later than civil law, by ANTONY AGOSTINI (1517-1586).[4] Son of the Vice-Chancellor of the Kingdom of Aragon, he learnt his law in Spain and then at Padua and Bologna, where he studied under Alciati and also Mariano Sozzini. First *auditor* then bishop in Italy and Spain, he was for the last ten years of his life Archbishop of Tarragona. In 1576 he edited the first four *compilationes antiquae,* and in Tarragona wrote a treatise on the emendation of Gratian's Decreta: though composed before the work of the official *correctores* (1584) it was published after. Antony was a great collector of texts, and his library went after his death in part to the Escorial and in part to the Vatican library.

170. Cujas, Coquille. — If the *mos italicus* (Italian style) continued to be precise and calm despite its more literary expression, it was otherwise with the *mos gallicus* in France. Here a lively contempt was fashionable, spiced with invective which to us seems merely vulgar, and directed both at contemporary rivals and above all at the past.

JAMES CUJAS (*Cujacius,* 1522-1590)[5] was the greatest exponent of this contempt for the past. He studied law at Toulouse, but thought too little of his masters to finish the course. Instead he set up on his own there in 1547 as a teacher of the Institutes, with great success. From 1554 to his death he was a salaried professor, mostly at Bourges,[6] and acquired a very great reputation for learning. His interest was in the reconstitution of Roman law before Justinian, Justinian's corpus being guilty in his eyes not only of impure latinity but also of fouling the limpid waters of classical law. Of his voluminous publications about half were posthumous.

---

2. B. KURTSCHEID, *Bartoli de Saxoferrato ... influxus,* (1938) 11 Apollinaris 110, 116.
3. 6 SAVIGNY 353; ZACCAGNINI, *Storia dello Studio di Bologna durante il Rinascimento* (1930), at page 205.
4. E. MAGNIN, (1935) 1 Naz 627.
5. M. PREVOST, (1961) 9 D.B.F. 1362.
6. He was first at Cahors for a year, and for two periods (1557 to 1559 and 1567 to 1575) in the Dauphiné, the first time apparently at Grenoble, and the second (Grenoble having been suppressed in 1565) at Valence. He also spent a year (1566-67) teaching at Turin.

This disregard of the present continued to be the attitude of the universities; but alongside it continued also comment by practitioners on the law as it actually was, more particularly the Customs.

The Custom of the Nivernais found its commentator in GUY COQUILLE (1523-1603)[7] who at the age of 20 heard the younger Mariano Sozzini at Padua. His doctorate however, in both laws, he took at Orléans in 1548, and began a career in local administration and at the bar in the Nivernais. In 1571 he became Procurator General of the province, and in 1590 published his Commentary. It was republished after his death, as were two other works, the *Institution* (introduction) *au Droit Français* (meaning customary law), and *Questions et Réponses sur les Coustumes de France*.

171. D'Argentré. — A few years older than both of these was BERTRAND D'ARGENTRÉ (*Argentraeus*, 1519-1590),[8] already a Breton separatist and feudalist when appointed Sénéchal at Rennes (1547) in succession to his father. Despite his radical opposition to Dumoulin's ideal of a single law and of royal supremacy over local lordlings, it is pleasing to record that Dumoulin "knew no more learned lawyer" than d'Argentré, and that d'Argentré frequently expressed his admiration for Dumoulin's intellectual qualities. It must be borne in mind that there is much more to the law than that, and in other branches not much separated them. In 1568 he published a Commentary on the first four Books of the old Custom of Brittany, and in 1584 on the Title "Donations" of the Old Custom. Meanwhile he served (from 1575) on the commission which drew the new Custom, promulgated in 1580. He had far more readers for his not too scrupulous History of Brittany (1582), and at the end of his life joined in the efforts of the League to make Brittany a base against King Henry of Navarre. This failing, he died of a broken heart in 1590.

Despite his classical Latin d'Argentré belonged to the past — indeed to the distant past, before the study of Roman law had begun to break down parochial boundaries. The future lay with Dumoulin, modern in every respect except his Latin.

172. England. — The Renaissance brought England back to a limited extent into the fold from which she had excluded herself in the thirteenth century. Canon law, it is true, had continued to be applied, and

7. M. PREVOST, (1961) 9 D.B.F. 581.
8. J. BALTEAU, (1939) 3 D.B.F. 572.

had even continued in a humble way to be taught; but when Lyndwood in 1430 or so published his *Provinciale* (a gloss on the provincial constitutions of Canterbury) his citations are all of continental writers, canonist and civilian: he found no single native writer worthy even of mention.[9] Part of King Henry VIII's religious revolution was the suppression of this academic study of canon law,[10] coupled with the revival (in 1535 at Oxford and in 1540 at Cambridge) of the teaching of civil law. THOMAS SMITH[11] (1513-1577), the first Regius professor of civil law at Cambridge, thought it right to equip himself with a continental doctorate, and accordingly spent two years at Paris, Orléans and Padua in which last university he obtained his degree after having listened to Alciati. On his return to Cambridge in 1542 he was "incorporated" as D.C.L. and taught from 1543 to 1549. But his principal activity was public life, and it was during an embassy to France from 1562 to 1564 that he wrote *de Republica Anglorum,* an account in English of the English constitution in Tudor times.

A good generation later Oxford received ALBERICO GENTILI[12] (1552-1608) in exile from Italy for his Protestantism. His Perugian doctorate of 1572 (his masters are known but are not noteworthy)[13] founded his "incorporation" at Oxford in 1580. During his ten years' teaching at Oxford he published his *de Juris Interpretibus Dialogi Sex* (1582), defending the older methods of legal study from the attacks of Cujas and other humanists; a treatise on diplomatic privilege (*de Legationibus,* 1585); and the first edition (1588) of his Law of War. From 1590 he was in practice at the admiralty and ecclesiastical bar in London: his notes on the cases in which he represented the King of Spain (published posthumously) are the earliest account of the law of prize; and his Law of War (his own final edition is of 1598) was the foundation for much of Grotius.

For it was not the humanists who sired modern law. It was those who defended the old learning, such as Alberico in public international law; or who were themselves exponents of it, such as Albert Gandini and Angelo of Arezzo in criminal law, and above all Dumoulin in civil law.

---

9. F.W. MAITLAND, *Roman Canon Law in the Church of England* (1898, pages 51 to 99 of *Church, State and Decretals*), page 98.
10. *Loc. cit.,* at page 92. And again *English Law and the Renaissance* (1901, reprinted at pages 135 to 151 of *Selected Historical Essays of F.W. Maitland,* edited by Helen CAM, 1957), at page 138.
11. A.F. POLLARD, (1898) 53 D.N.B. 124.
12. T.E. HOLLAND, (1890) 21 D.N.B. 124 [sic].
13. ERMINI, *Perugia,* at page 534.

Index

References are to the numbered paragraphs of the text, not to pages. Numbers separated by a colon refer to the paragraph and accompanying footnote. Within each entry the order is not alphabetical.